will be great in all you do 8/22/07

THE ANATOMY OF PROBLEM-SOLVING

TIM HOBBS

Hobbs Technical Consulting, LLC
PO Box 76026
Colorado Springs, CO 80970
www.hobbstech.com

ISBN: 1-4196-4697-3
or
ISBN 978-1-4196-4697-3

To order additional copies please contact us.

BookSurge, LLC
www.booksurge.com
1-866-308-6235

Contents

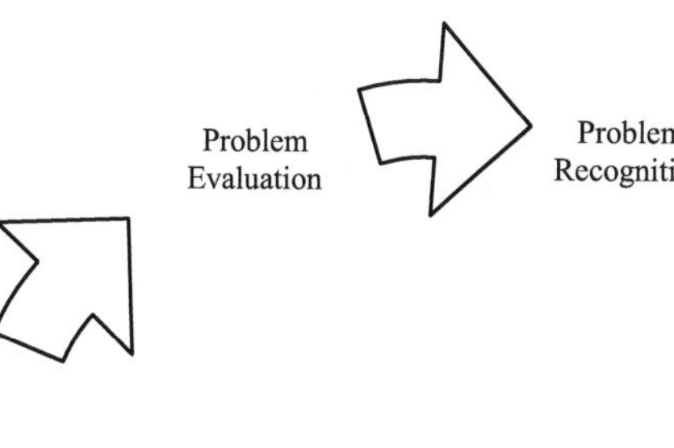

Introduction

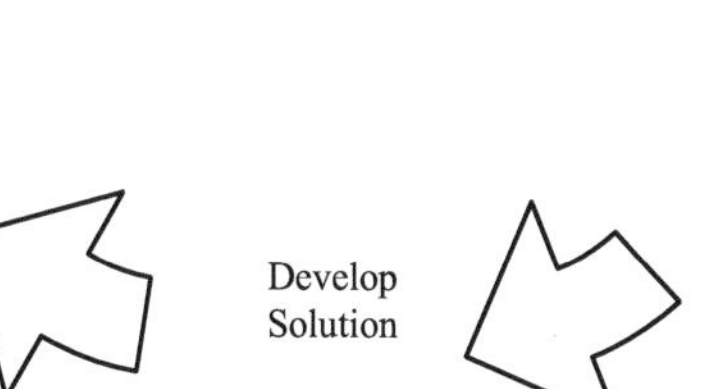

Acknowledgement

This book is dedicated to the memory of my mother, Mrs. Catherine Juanita Hobbs. I would also like to dedicate this book to my grandmother Ms. Elmina Corley. Your wisdom and prayers continue to mold my life.

I would like to thank my lovely wife Lashunder, Godmother Mrs. Marilyn Cuffee-Gordon and great friends Kimberly Green, Al Jones, James and Charlotte Wright for believing in my vision throughout the years. I also want to thank the many other friends and mentors throughout my career who have inspired me to publish this book.

Message from the Author

This problem-solving approach was introduced to me while in the Navy when I was 18 years old. As an eager and anxious young sailor, I thought I would never be able to repair anything. My first technical instructor said that if I could grasp the art of troubleshooting I would be able to repair anything from an average household item to a nuclear reactor. Guess what? He was correct. I have been using this problem-solving approach for almost 20 years with great success. There has not been a problem I have not been able to solve... how long it has taken is another story.

This process works! I have successfully used this approach throughout my career. If you have a passion for solving problems, you will enjoy this book. Many professional problem solvers use a similar process that is usually tailored to better meet their specific applications. For example, the medical profession relies on a similar approach to identify the treatment for illnesses and diseases. Criminal investigators use this approach to solve mysterious crimes. Throughout the years, I have tailored this process to fit various organizations and industries. Essentially it is the same basic process.

As a result of using this process, I was indirectly accused of sabotaging equipment and inducing problems prior to leaving work to elude my team. It was literally taking me only hours to solve the elusive problems that my peers had been troubleshooting around the clock for 3-4 days. My module engineers marveled at the speed and accuracy of my troubleshooting abilities. I was asked by my team regarding how I was able to solve some seemingly complex problems with such accuracy in a short amount of time. My answer was simple; I was troubleshooting. I was applying the problem-solving techniques and strategies that you are preparing to explore.

The following problem-solving process has been modified throughout my career to cover a variety of problems you may encounter ranging from simple home repairs, automobile failures, advanced high tech equipment and process problems. Embracing this process will save you time and money while enabling you to have a sense of pride in your ability to solve various problems.

I began utilizing this approach at home to ensure that I would be able to apply my troubleshooting approach to various applications. It made sense... right? I was saving my company millions of dollars throughout the years while still outsourcing simple home and automobile repairs. To my immediate surprise, I was able to make various household repairs that enabled me to rack up *brownie-points* with my then pregnant wife. My troubleshooting confidence increased the more I was able to perform routine repairs.

To further my confidence, I purchased a *hoopty* (84 Honda Accord) to learn how to make simple car repairs. A *hoopty* is an early model vehicle that is sure to have some problems. The cost of ownership will increase as the aging parts begin to fail. You see, I was completely ignorant when it came to repairing cars. I thought changing my oil was a great accomplishment. So to further educate and challenge myself, I purchased a Chilton manual for the model of my car. My hoopty experience taught me how to make simple car repairs.

Throughout this book, I will take you phase-by-phase into the world of advanced problem-solving techniques. I will explain the importance of root-cause problem-solving and its impacts on your career, job placement and the financial health of your organizations. We will conduct a thorough review of each phase in this process. I will offer many actual examples of *True Stories* I have encountered throughout my career. Finally, to reinforce this process, at the end of each chapter I will walk you systematically through a gas heating system problem I encountered while writing this book.

True Story: Tales of the Hoopty

My hoopty died on me twice during the three years I owned it. The first time the car died while I was driving on a back road with two of my kids. Fortunately, I was able to get a ride from a nice gentleman to meet my wife. After towing the car home, I was able to troubleshoot the problem to an improperly wired electrical system by a previous owner. A 30-amp fuse to the fuel pump was sharing the load with my heating system. Now the total load of the circuit was 40-amps. The problem manifested during my first winter when I turned on the heating system, which overloaded the circuit and blew the fuse. The second time the car died while traveling on an overpass bridge. I later troubleshot the problem and found an aging distributor cap that was misfiring. I had many other problems: a bad battery, low fluid in the clutch system, a mechanical linkage broke on the window motor, overheating due to an aging radiator and difficulty passing emissions tests. I actually ran out of fuel once. Don't laugh... ***Never assume****. The car was given a proper funeral after only one month of selling it for $600 to the next owner. I did not feel bad because he said he was* ***Hoopty Certified****.*

Problem-Solving is about Leadership

Leadership is the capacity to influence others through inspiration, motivated by a passion, generated by a vision, ignited by a purpose.

- Dr. Myles Monroe
Motivational Speaker

Strong leadership skills are essential for every expert team problem-solver. Your passion to solve problems must be apparent and contagious. You must be confident in your team's ability to effectively solve the problem at hand. I have learned that *it is difficult to lead people who don't trust you.* To be effective in leading teams you must:

- **Discover your purpose:** Why are we here? You must state clearly what the team's purpose is to avoid confusion. Primarily, the team is formed to solve a specific problem or to uncover an opportunity.

- **Generate a vision:** You must see this problem solved in your mind. Visualization is a great way to motivate yourself and your team. Most professional athletes and coaches such as Phil Jackson of the LA Lakers use the principles of visualization to motivate their teams before games. I'm not saying that you should get in a circle and hold hands… primarily; I'm suggesting more of a change of mindset or attitude.

- **Passion:** Your generated passion will be contagious to all those around you. Your ***failure-is-not-an-option*** attitude will motivate others to follow your lead. No job or task is too big or too small for you. If you begin to contribute long hours and become a ***go-for*** others will follow. A *go-for* is the person that will go for this… or go for that. Basically, this person will do what it takes to keep the progress of the team moving even if it means running small errands for others.

- **Inspiration:** As you begin to win your team's confidence you will be able to inspire them to be successful. You will be able to help them unleash their true potential to excel and to become innovative-thinkers towards solving the problem.

- **Influence:** You can successfully influence and lead those who you have been able to truly inspire.

Attributes of Effective Leaders:

- Leaders see problems as opportunities to be creative.
- Leaders embrace change.
- Leaders are natural change agents.
- Leaders are visionaries… they don't merely see things as they are but also what they can become.
- Leaders are like thermostats… they monitor and change the atmosphere.

Preface

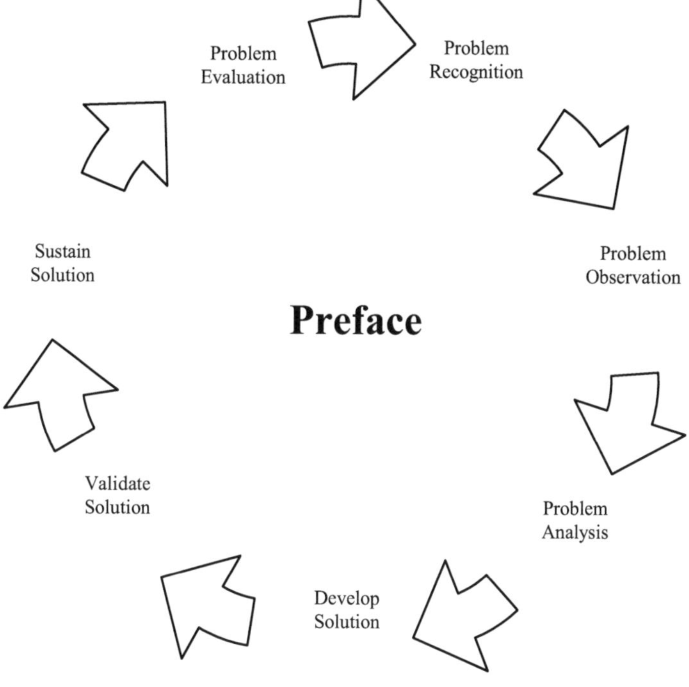
Problem Recognition
Problem Observation
Problem Analysis
Develop Solution
Validate Solution
Sustain Solution
Problem Evaluation

Preface

This book was written for those with a passion for solving problems as an individual or in a team environment. Regardless of what industry you find yourself working, you will have to learn the art of troubleshooting. This book and the accompanying workshops/seminars are designed to take the fear and mystery out of problem-solving. Throughout this book, I will intentionally interchange the words troubleshooting and problem-solving. In the context of this book they are the same.

Effectively solving problems is vastly different from fixing problems. If you only ***fix*** the problem, it will return because you did not properly eliminate the root-cause of the problem. If you effectively ***solve*** the problem, it will never return because you would have implemented the proper countermeasures to ensure that the failure is properly contained and resolved.

Many companies are struggling to maintain their competitive advantage. Companies are desperately trying to implement lean principles to remain cost competitive. Consequently, effectively solving problems has become an area of high interest in the high technology manufacturing sector.

In this book, I will take you through a process that many professionals are using to solve problems in various industries. You will learn proven techniques that will enable you to solve any problem that you may face as a professional problem-solver. More importantly, you will learn how to apply these skills in a team environment, which is how numerous companies prefer to solve problems. Team problem-solving can accelerate your problem-solving efforts. However, if not done properly it can become a massive barrier due to competing egos and a lack of synergy among team members.

Finally, it is my desire to bring the excitement and passion back into problem-solving. Most people are intimidated by some of the problems that they face. I have learned that a majority of people when asked admit that they have never been formally trained to effectively solve problems in a team environment.

Why should a non-technical person read this book?

I guess I should ask you… do you own a home or a car. Have you ever been helplessly stranded beside the road because your car *broke-down?* Are you terrified to take your car to the mechanic because you think they will overcharge you for work that you don't need at this time? Have you ever been tasked to lead a problem team through a difficult problem? Have you ever been assigned to work on a team-problem that appeared to have no clear objectives or leadership? Do you desire to be able to solve complex problems with confidence? If you have answered yes to any of these questions then this book will be beneficial to you.

This book is not designed to impress you with my technical knowledge, but rather to introduce you to the realm of advanced problem-solving through the use of technical illustrations. I chose technical problems because they are easy to evaluate… *no gray areas here.* Either it works or it doesn't. Non-technical problems can oftentimes be too *touchy-feely.* For example, how do measure if you have increased the morale of your employees by 20%. Most business problems are complicated to evaluate because of office *politics.* For instance, how do we get people to buy more of our products? It is easy to measure the progression of business-technical problems. For example, we can measure if we have increased equipment availability by 30% for four consecutive weeks.

Why the high-tech manufacturing industry?

Why not? The high-tech manufacturing industry has to be one of the most difficult and challenging industries to work in. Technical professionals are tasked to solve complex problems. The high tech industry attracts some of the brightest minds. When you are working on cutting edge proprietary technology, who are you going to call when your process goes awry? One manufacturing process excursion can have a detrimental affect on your revenues. One maintenance accident could result into a major environmental hazard, equipment damage, process excursion or a fatality. The average selling price of products is unpredictable. In fact, the prices of personal computers (PC's), cell-phones and laptops are constantly dropping to remain cost competitive.

So if companies have access to the same technical resources and average selling prices are constantly getting lower, how do companies compete? A company must effectively utilize their resources, execute to their strategies, and solve problems to remain competitive. If I can teach you how to solve problems within this industry, you should be able to successfully apply this approach to your area of expertise.

Why Phases and not Steps?

In my opinion, to refer to this process in steps does not truly capture the innovative thinking that must occur to successfully solve difficult problems. Steps are simply defined by Webster as *stages in a series*.

For example: **My Morning Routine**

1. Alarm goes off 4:30 a.m.
2. Get out of bed 4:45 a.m.
3. Brush my teeth 4:50 a.m.
4. Shave 5:00 a.m.
5. Shower 5:10 a.m.
6. Get dressed 5:15 a.m.
7. Eat breakfast 5:30 a.m.
8. Off to work 6:00 a.m.

As you can see, there is not a lot of thought that goes into my mornings; it's very structured. No major decisions are required. I can easily substitute or replace these steps to meet my goal, which is to leave my home no later than 6:00 am.

A **phase** is *defined as a distinguishable part of a process*. A process is defined as a series of actions leading to a particular result. This definition truly captures the uniqueness of the process/approach that you will learn throughout this book. Each phase will challenge you to examine the problem in a unique way. No phase in the process can be excluded or rearranged. However, the strategies I recommend within the phases can be customized to fit your situation.

Why the title? The Anatomy of Problem-Solving

To be honest, the title came to me after I wrote the book while watching a forensic crime show; my favorite past-time activity. I have always been fascinated with crime investigation shows. I enjoy evaluating how forensic scientists are able to process evidence from a crime scene to aid investigators. One particular show was titled *The Anatomy of a Crime.* During the show the viewers were able to actually re-live the crime with the host. The techniques utilized were similar to what I learned as a technical problem-solver. The word *anatomy* caught my attention like a bolt of lightning.

After looking up the definition I was sold on the title. One of the definitions for the word *anatomy* is defined as a detailed explanation or analysis. I did not want to simply provide techniques to solve problems but offer a detailed analysis of problem-solving. Oftentimes solving the problem requires more than just technical knowledge. In addition, you need to understand how to work in a team environment and how to lead others through difficulties. Sometimes the attitude of the team can become a problem. It is my desire to help you to look at problems from various points of views.

The Anatomy of Problem-Solving Purpose

1. To provide some insight to the upcoming challenges that we are facing today in the workforce:

    - Aging workforce
    - Skilled-worker shortage
    - Knowledge gaps
    - Volatile economy

2. Provide some strategies that organization's can apply to successfully overcome these challenges.

3. Systematically walk the reader through the *Anatomy of Problem-Solving* principles one phase at a time.

4. Offer readers true-story examples to emphasize the recommended strategies that are suggested throughout the book.

5. Methodically walk the reader through a non-threatening problem to solve through each phase of the process.

6. Offer readers real-world strategies to apply to their everyday problem-solving challenges.

7. Provide the reader with some thought provoking remarks and quotes to help them navigate through their career.

8. Prepare the next generation of problem-solvers for future workforce challenges.

9. To bring the fun and passion back into problem-solving.

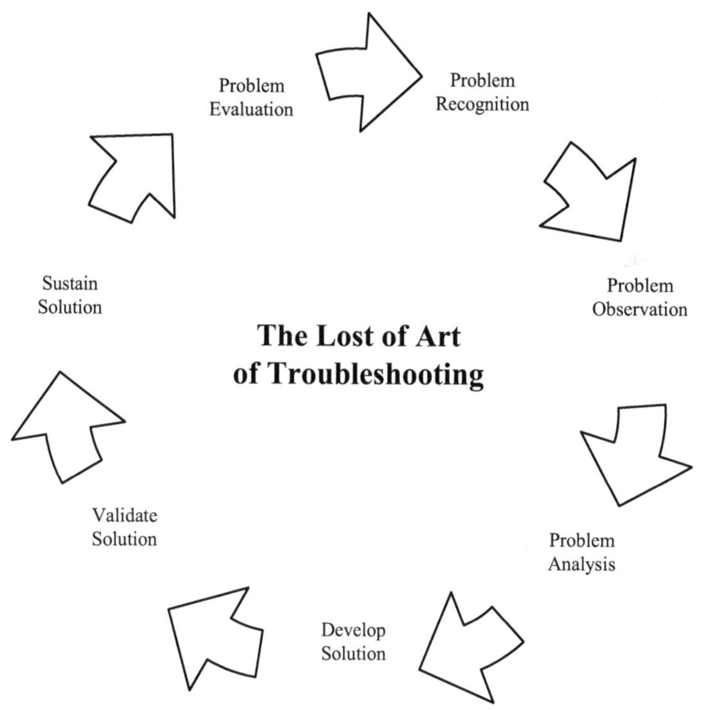
Problem
Evaluation
Problem
Recognition
Problem
Observation
Problem
Analysis
Develop
Solution
Validate
Solution
Sustain
Solution
The Lost of Art
of Troubleshooting

Chapter 1

The Lost Art of Troubleshooting

Observation is the key to transformation.
- ***Unknown***

Troubleshooting is quickly becoming a lost art. The technical community is becoming more and more dependent upon automated systems oftentimes referred to as built-in-test-equipment (BITE) to assist in troubleshooting. Though highly useful, these systems can usually only detect the first place of failure or the manifestation of the problem. For example, an increased temperature in your body is an indication that your body's defense mechanism has kicked into gear to fight an infection. Many technical professionals have become too reliant on these systems. What if the automated diagnosis is incorrect? These systems usually can't detect a loose wire that is intermittently making a poor connection.

In this chapter we will begin to explore some reasons why problem-solving is becoming a lost art. I will present some alarming statistics regarding various industries within the U.S. We will begin to explore some key questions and observations regarding how we arrived at our current situation.

What's the Big Deal?

In a volatile economy, it is becoming extremely difficult for many companies to maintain their competitive advantage. Major companies within the high-tech manufacturing industries are coming under insurmountable pressure to accurately forecast quarterly earnings to their shareholders. The cost of manufacturing is continuously increasing due to the rise in operational cost. Primarily, this increase is caused by expensive repairs and an increase of equipment downtime due to ineffective troubleshooting. To make matters worse, the industries are also beginning to experience a knowledge-gap due to an aging workforce.

The National Association for Colleges and Employees (NACE) predicts that a majority of educational institutions are not properly preparing the next generation of technicians and engineers for the future challenges. As a result, employers are having difficulty finding qualified candidates to meet these challenges. (NACE, 2005) In a *Voice of America* article by Faiza Elmasry, she stated that employers are expecting graduates to have a degree, but also some professional experience and general skills. (Elmasry, 2005)

In the next 10 years, industry analysts are predicting a 40-70% loss of maintenance personnel in the marketplace. The National Association of Manufacturers (NAM) is on the frontlines declaring that this problem will become a national epidemic if we do not develop an effective strategy to properly educate the next generation of manufacturing employees. In a survey conducted in 2001, 80% of all manufacturers surveyed reported a shortage of qualified manufacturing workers in the next 10-20 years. NAM also estimates that in the next 20 years over 76 million baby boomers will be leaving the workforce with only 46 million generation X'ers on the horizon. Some analysts believe that we have already begun to experience the affects. (National Association of Manufacturing, 2001)

How Did We Get Here?

I have been helplessly observing this problem occurring over the last 10 years in the high-tech manufacturing industry. This problem evolved in three phases. I will briefly explain each of these phases to offer some insight to where we are quickly heading. I will also give you an overall analysis so that you can get a better grasp of this problem. These phases are cyclical as a result of our volatile economy.

High-Tech Manufacturing Industry

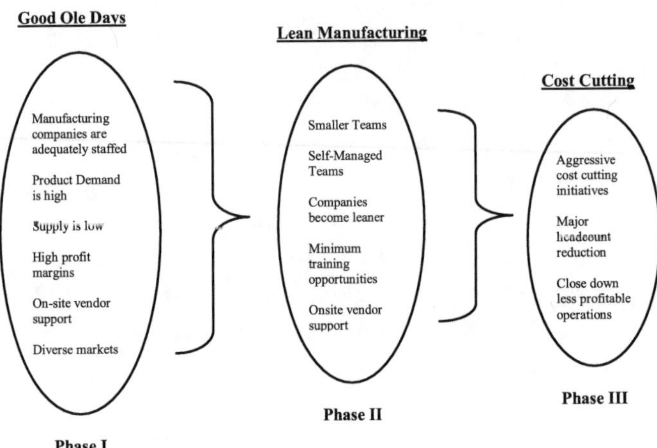

Diagram 1

Phase I - The Good Ole Days

Many high-tech companies were experiencing huge profits margins in the early 90's. The demand for computing products exceeded the supply. Manufacturing teams were usually overstaffed to meet the challenges during this phase; oftentimes with under qualified technicians. On-site vendors were available around the clock to ensure that the manufacturing equipment was always ready to move product through the lines. Operation cost was not a major focus due to high profit margins. As a result, spare parts were readily available. There were unlimited training opportunities for company employees.

Phase II - Lean Manufacturing

In the late 90's, product demand began to fall and profit margins were decreasing. As a result, many manufacturers in the high-tech industry began to adopt rival Japanese companies' lean manufacturing productivity models. Lean manufacturing strategies enabled U.S. companies to streamline their productivity models in an effort to reduce their enormous operational cost that was a carry-over from the *good-ole days*. Accordingly, training funds were carefully scrutinized due to the high cost and poor performance of formally trained employees. Some companies sought to combine employee roles to improve their productivity models. On-site field service engineers remained on-site for critical manufacturing equipment; however, the quality of support began to dwindle. In addition, most major customers began to adopt the *Just-in-Time* manufacturing schemes of Dell, which resulted in a reduction of inventory.

Phase III - Cost Cutting

The bottom finally fell out in 2000 as the U.S. began to feel the economic pressures of a recession. We also began to experience our nation's worst case of corporate scandals. To make matters worse, on September 11, 2001 we witnessed the worst terrorist event every to occur on American soil with the fall of New York's famous Twin Towers that claimed almost 3,000 innocent lives. As a result, consumer confidence was severely shaken. Companies large and small were not eager to invest in the next generation of computing products. Aggressive cost cutting strategies were being implemented to remain profitable. Due to high cost, on-site vendor contracts, off-site training and spare parts inventory became easy targets. Many companies began to close the doors of unprofitable operations and businesses to remain cost competitive.

Overall High-Tech Industry Analysis

The lean manufacturing strategy was only temporarily successful. Many companies cut too deep into their headcount resulting in a loss of many skilled employees. Off-site vendor training did not adequately prepare the manufacturing technicians to perform advanced equipment problem-solving. Unknown too many senior managers, the on-site field service engineers were performing most of the advanced equipment problem-solving. Recent college graduates were taking too long to train due to a lack of real-world experience. Peer-to-peer training was ineffective due to the poor equipment or system knowledge of trainers. Financial resources were limited because of aggressive cost cutting strategies, which were also contributing to a strain on the remaining resources. Product life cycles became shorter, thus greatly reducing the profitability window.

Most seasoned technicians and engineers were also being promoted to advance their careers or were heading for retirement resulting in a huge knowledge-skills gap. Those departing would be taking an abundance of undocumented techniques that had been learned throughout the years; commonly referred to as ***tribal knowledge***. As a result, the already struggling companies began to suffer many quality excursions, poor equipment availability and a spike in operation cost.

What does the manufacturing industry look like?

- *Volatile economy* - A volatile economy is making it difficult for organizations to accurately forecast revenue trends.

- *Smaller teams* - As organizations are becoming leaner, teams are becoming smaller. However, the goals are becoming more challenging.

- *Just-In-Time (JIT) manufacturing* - Manufacturing facilities are trying to accurately forecast product demand, thus only manufacturing product in a Just-In-Time manner.

- *Cost-cutting initiatives* - Organizations are eagerly trying to find ways to reduce operational cost and to increase profit margins.

- *Excessive tool downtime* - Excessive equipment downtime is directly impacting an organization's ability to control maintenance cost and increase revenue.

- *Ineffective team problem-solving* - Organizations are trying to establish 24-hour troubleshooting strategies to meet current and future challenges.

What does the manufacturing industry want?

- *Enhance economies of scale* - Organizations desire to do more with less. This is not impossible to accomplish.

- *Self-managed teams* - These teams are assembled with highly qualified and motivated employees who require minimum supervision.

- *Empowered employees* - When employees are empowered they are allowed to share in the ownership of a particular job. These motivated employees are allowed to be creative within reason to accomplish their goals.

- *Knowledge-workers* - Today's technical professionals need to be highly trained on various aspects of a particular job. Simply knowing how to repair a piece of equipment is not good enough.

    - The next generation of technical professionals need to be able to:

        - Multi-task efficiently.
        - Comprehend basic computer and network functions.
        - Solve problems in a team environment.

- Comprehend the cost of downtime.
- Be technically trainable.
- Streamline preventive maintenance procedures.
- Develop innovative strategies and techniques to solve problems.
- Develop and manage projects.

U.S. Manufacturing Industry Facts:

- **Aging Workforce** - Recent studies of various technical industries indicate that in the next 10 years an aging technical workforce will be nearing retirement. In 2014 it is estimated that 78 million baby-boomers will be retiring. Unfortunately, these seasoned technicians and engineers will take a lot of undocumented knowledge with them.

- **Education training gap** - Other observations also indicate that recent college graduates and organizations are not adequately prepared to immediately close this gap. In 1996, Motorola turned away 90% of its applicants. (Messmer, 1996)

- **Lack of skilled workers** - A survey of 360 manufacturing companies reported that 50% had a deficiency in problem-solving skills among employees. 38% of the nation's largest companies surveyed reported that it is difficult to find skilled-workers; the situation worsens for engineers and technicians. (Messmer, 1996)

- **Missing the mark -** *10 years later...* In a new study released in January 2006 by "The National Survey of America's College Students" funded by Pew Charitable Trusts, it was estimated that more than 50% of 2 and 4 year college students lack the skills to perform complex literacy skills. Over 20% of college students lack basic quantitative literacy skills such as those required to compare ticket prices. Dr. Stephan Baldi, a principle research scientist for the American Institute for Research who directed the study, says…

"*The surprisingly weak quantitative literacy ability of many college graduates is troubling. A knowledgeable workforce is vital to cope with the increasing demands of the global marketplace.*" – **Dr. Stephan Baldi**

- **Ineffective equipment maintenance** - Various studies also indicate that 70% of equipment problems are self-induced. Most companies are operating at 10-40% efficiency. (Leonard, 2005)

What is the *Anatomy of Problem-Solving* Approach?

The Anatomy of Problem-Solving is a safe systematic approach to solving problems in a team environment. This book will offer its readers the ability to combine theoretical practical ideas with true stories of real problems to reinforce learning. *I define effective problem-solving as the successful identification, elimination and prevention of problems.*

The Anatomy of Problem-Solving Principles

1. Problem Recognition - Define the problem

2. Problem Observation - Clarify the current situation

3. Problem Analysis - Thoroughly analyze all data

4. Develop Solution - Design plan of action

5. Validate Solution - Analyze results

6. Sustain Solution - Sustain solutions

7. Problem Evaluation - Evaluation and follow up

- Each phase is uniquely different, but all are a vital piece of a mystery.
- Each phase is equally important.
- No phase should be ignored.

Benefits of this method

- *Continuous improvement* - Consistently utilizing this method to solve problems will enable companies to put real solutions in place to stop problems from re-occurring.

- *Increase training ROI (Return-on-investment)* - Individuals will be able to immediately apply this problem-solving approach that will positively impact their companies' bottom line by improving equipment availability and reducing maintenance cost.

- *Reduce the hidden cost of downtime* - Maintenance teams will be able to identify areas of opportunity to reduce nonscheduled equipment downtime and the cost of tool recovery.

- *Streamline maintenance plans* - Maintenance plans can be modified to improve equipment performance.

- *Root-cause analysis* - Individuals will learn how to apply innovative strategies designed to prevent problems from re-occurring.

Advantages of embracing the principles

You will have the ability to identify the root-cause of any problem. Root-cause problem-solving is vastly different from the *quick-fix* approach. The *quick-fix* approach usually results in undocumented procedures, or *tribal-knowledge* and high repair cost.

You will be able to recognize multiple problems. Oftentimes many problems are disguised and deceptive in nature. Technical professionals must be able to adequately identify multiple problems and categorize them as ***A*** problem vs. ***The*** problem.

***THE** Problem - has a direct impact on the problem you are confronting.*

***A** Problem - does not have a direct impact on the problem at hand, but if left unattended it will become **THE** problem of the future.*

For example, if you are troubleshooting a power failure you may discover that a power indicator lamp has failed. A burnt-out power lamp indicator is a problem, but does not determine if the system will receive power or not. A faulty lamp indicator is **A** problem. However, a blown fuse in the same power circuit will most likely be **The** problem, though it does not explain **why** the fuse failed. We will discuss this topic in more detail later in the book.

You will learn to remain on task and avoid Shot-gunning, Easter-egging and Swaptronics techniques which are extremely costly to a company. Throughout my technical career I have heard of many humorous gestures that relate to ineffective troubleshooting. All these examples resulted in a similar conclusion; a waste of company resources. Upon completion of this book you will be able to immediately identify when you have witnessed or become victim to one of these situations.

- ***Shot-gunning*** – To eagerly pursue the first idea that flies up with very little supporting data.

- ***Easter-egging*** – To aimlessly pursue a solution to a problem without any supporting data.

- ***Swaptronics*** – To replace components within your system without any supporting data or a true understanding of its impact.

- ***Rabbit Trails*** – Are similar to traveling through a maze; every path looks good but usually leads no-where.

*You will learn how to use all the available resources enabling you to **work smarter; not harder**.* Resources are precious commodities. Oftentimes many technical professionals are guilty of not properly utilizing all their available resources. As a result, they tend to *work harder rather than smarter.*

You will learn to exercise this approach every time you begin to troubleshoot a problem. Regardless of the type of problem you are solving, your desired outcome should be to effectively solve the problem the first time. I have heard it stated this way... *time is money and money is time.*

Oftentimes many problems are induced by careless troubleshooting efforts. Don't let the pressure to get a system back in service prevent you from using this method. *Short-cuts* usually lead to unsafe practices and extra cost.

The difference between people who succeed or fail is their ability to handle pressure.

- ***Edwin Lewis Cole***
Motivational Speaker

The ability to handle pressure is the key to solving complex problems. The seasoned problem-solver must remain calm to be able to lead teams to uncover the root-cause of the issue. *Calmness is contagious during a crisis.*

Why should you use this approach?

Other problems may be induced by improper troubleshooting methods. As we have previously discussed, ineffective troubleshooting approaches will most often delay your repair effort and increase the overall cost of downtime. Hasty troubleshooting approaches can exaggerate existing problems and potentially add new ones.

Some repairs are easy to perform. If the appropriate steps are conducted, the original problem is often easy to identify and repair. If a hasty approach is applied, it can take days, weeks, or even months to properly analyze what happened.

True Story: Faulty Repair Loop

Never assume *that a part you replaced is working correctly. Test every part that you replace to ensure accurate functionality. For example, while troubleshooting a system, I received four faulty parts over a two-week period. After reviewing all the historical data regarding the work that was* *previously performed, I was able to expose a faulty repair loop for these parts. After later conducting a more thorough investigation, I discovered that all the suspected parts were sent to the same calibration /repair lab. The lab was actually decommissioned, resulting in all the parts simply being re-inserted back into the parts system... of course for a small fee.*

******CAUTION******

Avoid the temptation to jump into the ***solution-space****. Many inexperienced problem-solvers would love to skip phases, presuming that they will be able to circumvent the problem quicker. The truth is that their actions usually result in greater frustration, more downtime, and increased repair cost.*

The person without an organized system of thought will always be at the mercy of the person who has one.
- Edwin Lewis Cole

People have the tendency to seek-out individuals who have the specific skills that they lack. For example, I visit my dentist when my teeth are aching for unexplained reasons. My dentist has the skills and the knowledge to properly analyze my discomfort. In the same way, your peers will begin to seek you out for your assistance during difficult times.

At first glance, the process may seem to be overkill to some. They may feel this process doesn't fit their style. They may also feel constrained and that their expertise is questioned. Actually, the process itself is very logical and easy to use for all problems – simple and complex irregardless of what industry or career you find yourself.

Early in my career, some of my peers did not value this approach. They proclaimed that the approach was too time consuming, ignoring the fact that I was consistently demonstrating its success.

The value of this approach will be evident as you use it and experience these results: high confidence in your ability to solve problems, decreased equipment downtime, reduced maintenance cost, increased equipment availability, and improved product quality... not to mention your ability to shine during performance evaluations and job interviews. Mastering how to recognize and solve problems will be your best career investment.

Okay... let's get into the material.

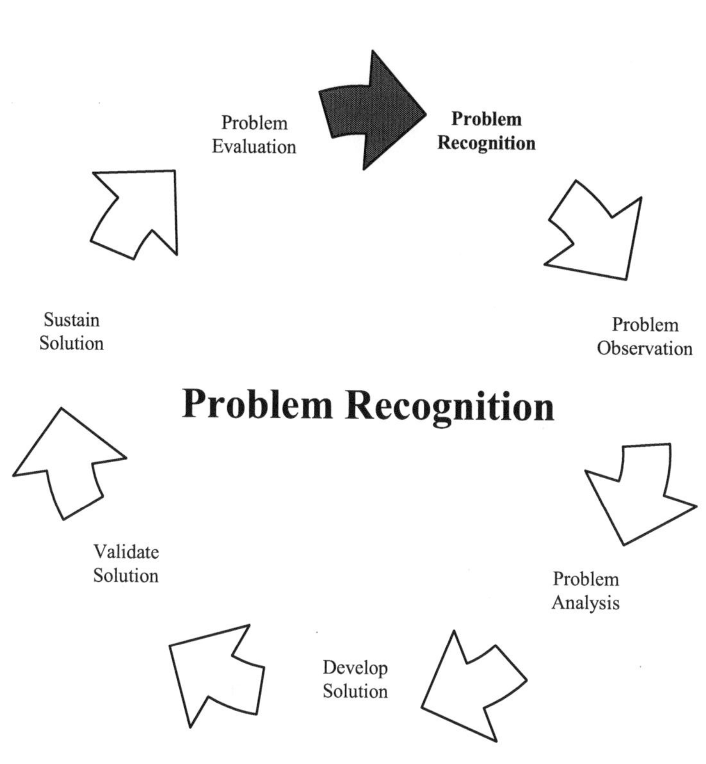
Problem
Evaluation
Problem
Recognition
Problem
Observation
Sustain
Solution
Problem Recognition
Validate
Solution
Problem
Analysis
Develop
Solution

Chapter 2

Problem Recognition

A problem improperly defined is poorly solved.

What is our objective? Why are we here? What is the impact?

It is imperative that you begin this process with the end in mind to guarantee a synergetic effort among your team. Precisely defining the problem or opportunity to explore is essential to the problem team's success. Your intended objectives and expected results should be accurately communicated. Accurately assessing the business impact of your problem will establish the *sense of urgency* for resolving the issue in a timely manner. Failing to set the tone for the problem-solving team is similar to a plane leaving Los Angeles heading to Hawaii with a one degree error within its onboard compass. A one degree error at departure will cause the plane to skew farther away from its Hawaiian destination resulting in some very unhappy passengers. During the *Problem Recognition* phase, you will learn how to correctly establish a solid foundation to your problem-solving efforts.

What is the sense of urgency?

What may be important to you may not be important to others. As a manager or leader it is essential to recognize your problem and establish your intended objectives early in the *Problem Recognition* phase. Accurately communicate *the sense of urgency* you want dedicated to this problem. As a result, you may have to de-prioritize other projects or efforts to guarantee success and to avoid overloading. Determining the sense of urgency will also help you determine what resources you may need to solve the problem. You may determine that you need a joint departmental effort for integrated problems or additional staffing requirements.

Do you have the correct skills available?

Carefully consider the skills that you need to properly investigate and resolve this issue prior to assembling a problem team. For example, if the business impact of the problem is low, the problem could be assigned to a junior engineer to help them develop their leadership effectiveness. After completing your skills assessment for the problem, begin to assign individuals to the problem team. Ensure that the problem team is balanced to promote a harmonious effort among the team. Duplicating skill-sets usually causes conflicts within your team due to various opposing styles. For example, why would you have two managers managing the same problem? You should conduct a skills assessment even if you are working alone. You may not have the necessary skills to accurately solve the problem.

True Story: Don't judge a book by its cover

Recently I experienced a problem with my garage door. The door would not properly open, which was causing a lot of stress at my house as my wife was trying to get the kids to school. As a responsible husband, I quickly went home to assess the situation and noticed that one of the two huge garage door springs was broken. At first glance, I thought this would be a relatively simple repair. After conducting a ***safety assessment*** *of the work required to replace the springs, I quickly recognized that I did not have the skills, tools, or the parts to safely conduct this repair. At the urging of my wife, I conceded and called a garage door expert to solve the problem. He commended me on my willingness to call for help on this repair. He said oftentimes when he arrives to a trouble call it is after some he-man determined that he can do the job.*

As a result of the high tension that is placed on the springs, the moment the spring tension is released, parts began to fly all over the place including pieces of the he-man who did not conduct a skills or safety assessment of the situation.

Look before you Leap
- Unknown

Who is responsible for managing the problem-solving effort?

In other words, who is going to guarantee that everyone adheres to the agreed upon proper problem-solving approach? This is not "*Da-Man*", but rather the individual responsible for properly managing the problem to resolution. I refer to this individual as the *problem-owner*. The problem-owner will be responsible for ensuring that all relevant documents or information are collected to ensure that everyone has a good understanding of the problem. They help to identify all the risks associated with the safe resolution of the problem. The problem-owner will establish the communication schemes such as determining the frequency of progress-update meetings. The problem-owner should seek to properly understand and define the team members' roles and responsibilities to avoid confusion later. It is also the problem-owner's responsibility to comprehend the team's ground rules and boundary conditions. Establishing ground rules and boundary conditions allows the team to determine how they will govern themselves throughout the problem-solving effort. My favorite ground-rule is *what is said behind closed doors stays behind closed doors*. This rule helps foster open and honest communication. The problem-owner is responsible for acting as a coach and mentor to the team. They primarily schedule and facilitate the problem team meetings. They also help manage internal conflicts among the team members. Finally, the problem-owner is responsible for comprehending the business impacts of the problem.

Assigning problem-owners in a team environment is a great approach to give others an opportunity to demonstrate their leadership and problem-solving skills. Delegating tasks to various junior technicians and engineers gives the senior technical experts the ability to monitor the progression of several problems without having to do all the *leg work.*

****** CAUTION ******

Many troubleshooting efforts are not effective because there is very little time allocated to structuring the problem-solving approach. High agreement is essential in a team troubleshooting effort. Multiple problems are overlooked during this phase and will most likely lead you down some endless ***rabbit trails****.*

Can two walk together, except they be agreed?
– Amos 3:3 (Bible, KJV)

Are you working on the correct problem?

Sometimes you will find yourself working on a problem that morphs into other sub-problems. As a problem team leader, you must decide which problem to solve that will give your team the greatest opportunity to meet your business objectives. For example, if as a medical professional you diagnose that your patient has: chest pains, a sinus infection, and an in-grown toe-nail. Which of the three problems will you address first? Most likely, you will choose to resolve the chest pains due to its impact on the whole body. *You don't want to put a band-aid on an open chest wound.* Once again, seek high agreement within your team to avoid internal conflicts later. What appears to be the simple problem is not the best problem to solve first. All potential problems must be evaluated to determine their impact to your business objectives. Consider the following true story.

True Story: Choose Your Battles Wisely

During one occasion, I was assigned by senior management to a focus group to assist a struggling module. The module struggled to maintain their equipment availability commitment that was impacting the organization's ability to satisfy current and future customer product demands. We uncovered several problems that needed to be addressed during our initial observation:

1. ***Major safety incidents** - Four weeks of downtime per incident.*

2. ***Tool qualifications** - Three days of downtime per event.*

3. ***Tool awaiting spare parts** - Two days of downtime per incident if parts are not available on site.*

4. ***Tool awaiting technical support** - Due to limited human resources.*

5. ***Ambiguous procedures** - Procedures were poorly documented preventing consistency from technician-to-technician.*

6. ***Lack of trained technicians** - Technicians were inducing other problems due to improper troubleshooting methods.*

The problem team decided to focus on issues 1-3 due to their impact on our equipment availability. We were given six months to solve this problem. Because of our synergetic focused effort, we were able to improve the equipment availability by 30% within three months, which exceeded our availability goals.

The Problem Team Structure

My most productive teams consisted of 6-8 key stakeholders. From my experience, if the team is too small it will be unable to accurately analyze the problem in a timely manner because it will lack the necessary skill-sets. On the other hand, if the team is too large due to redundant roles the team may get bogged down. Various opposing opinions could cause the team to become paralyzed. *The problem team is designed to have tension.* Each stakeholder is responsible for their own interest ensuring the best solution is selected to meet the team's objectives.

- ***The manager-in-charge*** is primarily responsible for the strategic success of the team. The manager in charge selects the primary team members and selects the problem-owner. They establish the boundary conditions and determine the *sense of urgency* of the problem. Usually the manager-in-charge will also be the tie-breaker if the team gets into a troublesome situation such as resolving team conflicts or re-negotiating boundary conditions.

- ***The problem-owner*** is primarily responsible for the tactical success of the team. They consult regularly with the *manager-in-charge*. They also assume the role as the coach and mentor of the team.

- ***The senior process or product expert*** is the individual who has the most process experience with respect to the problem. They will help determine the actual process and product impacts of the team's efforts. They are normally the primary data extractor for the group.

- ***The senior equipment expert*** is the individual who has the most equipment experience for the suspect system. This individual is responsible for collecting relevant documents and educating the team on the theories of operations, safety, and system performance. This individual is primarily responsible for organizing actual plans or tasks to be performed.

- ***The supervisor*** is responsible for managing and assigning the individual resources and determining product shipment implications of the team's proposed solutions.

- ***The technical expert*** is the individual responsible for actually performing the work of the team. Their perspective enables the team to quickly determine the feasibility of the proposed solutions.

Clearly define or describe the problem(s) as you understand it.

Defining or describing a problem in one statement as a team is not as easy as you think. *It's not working right...* is not good enough. Usually an experienced problem-solver will ask you to be a little more specific by asking you a series of questions based upon previous knowledge regarding the alleged problem. Developing a problem statement is not necessary to many anxious technicians and engineers because they have ***Real*** work to do. However, in a team environment in which many will have an opportunity to participate during the problem effort, it would behoove you to *take the time vs. spending the time later*. It doesn't take long to lose control of a simple problem. When working in a team environment, ensure that you reach ***high-agreement*** of exactly what the problem is before launching into an aggressive problem-solving effort.

Pay me now or pay me later.

I recall many times after numerous failed attempts to solve a problem that some members on the team had different ideas of what the problem actually was. As a result, the team was simply going in circles. At best, we were counter productive.

A problem statement can be as simple as:

- *The heater system is not heating and is making a loud noise.*
- *The equipment is experiencing intermittent gas alarms.*
- *The car will not crank when it is cold.*
- *The hot water is not getting hot.*
- *The module is not meeting equipment availability goals.*

As more information is uncovered after a thorough investigation is conducted, the problem statement will most likely be revised. In the case of the faulty heater system example above, you may later discover that the gas valve was turned off. However, that does not explain from where the loud noise is coming.

Do you thoroughly comprehend the functionality of the system or process?

This is one of the most overlooked steps in troubleshooting or general problem-solving. It is difficult to determine what is not working correctly if you do not have a clear understanding of how it was designed to work. This is known as *the theory of operation or the process flow.*

The *theory of operation* is simply a technical or detailed description that explains the actual theories that were used to design a system such as electrical or mechanical laws. This is a great time to gather all the documentation, including manuals and specifications, regarding the problem. In my experience, it is better to review the material alone or as a team to better comprehend how the system is designed to work. I can recall many times spending several hours reading various manuals in the cafeteria or quietly at my desk. I became a sponge for knowledge during the initial year of my high-tech career. I was absorbing a lot of information that I would later use as the foundation of my career. It was important to my success to fully understand how to solve extremely challenging problems in a team environment.

For example: Ohm's law defines the relationship between Power, Current, Resistance and Voltage. Ohm's law consists of several equations to define electrical relationships.

A popular equation is $\boldsymbol{E = I\,R}$ (Voltage drop = Current * Resistance)

- **DC power supply**- a standard DC power supply electronic circuit is designed to do the following:
    - step power up or down by the use of a transformer
    - convert AC to DC with the use of diodes (half or full wave rectifiers)
    - filter out noise with the use of capacitors
    - voltage is regulated with the use of transistors

The goal of the system is to simply produce a regulated source of desired power. Each block within the basic block diagram can utilize several theories to accomplish the desired output.

Basic DC Power Supply

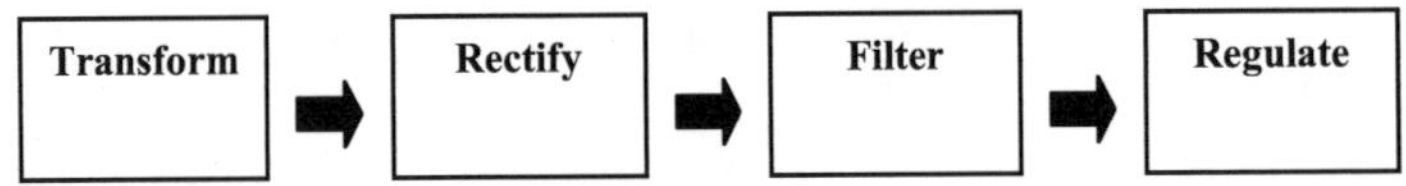

Diagram 1-1

Most electronic equipment in your home or office contains a DC power supply that will transform 120 vac (voltage alternating current) to a specified vdc (voltage direct current) operating voltage to meet various electronic applications required for CD players and computers. A failure of either of these blocks will prevent the system from producing the desired power output. Through various testing techniques you will be able to determine which block is not performing properly. .

True Story: Job Interview

During my first technical job interview I was shown a diagram of a DC power supply in the form of an electrical schematic. I was asked a very generic question such as, ***what is this.*** *My panel interviewers were amazed at a sudden moment of silence ... assuming that I was stumped on the very first question as I was trying to determine what the circuit was. My answer stunned them when I confidently stated...* ***This is a power supply****. What I did not notice was that the interviewer was only pointing to the first component of the power supply, which was a transformer. The interviewer's intent was to ask me a series of questions regarding each component and purpose of each block to determine if I had any idea of how a power supply operated. My answer clearly demonstrated my technical ability to understand how a power supply operated. Because of the interview, I started at a higher pay grade than my peers who also were interviewed at that time.*

You only get one time to make a first impression.

The following is an example of a system block diagram, system description and its theory of operation. System block diagrams, similar to process flow diagrams, reveal the inter-dependency of each block. A *basic closed-loop* diagram is the foundation of most equipment systems that require the ability to control an output. Control systems are similar to an air conditioning system. For instance, if you set the control setting to 60 degrees Fahrenheit, you expect it to stay there. Anything more or less would imply that your system is not functioning properly.

Basic Closed-loop Diagram Illustration

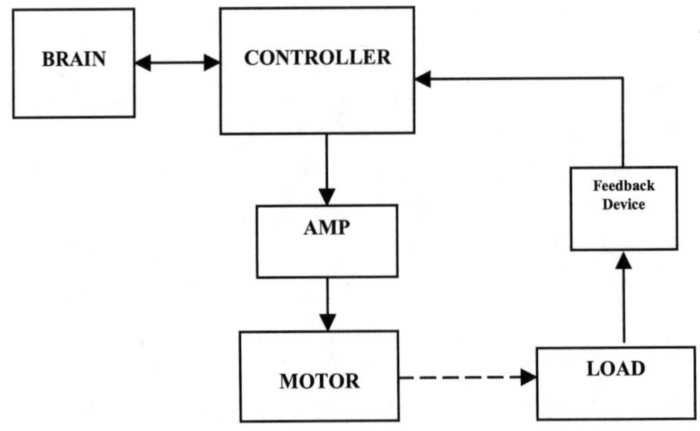

Diagram 1-2

Objective: To control load set points.

1. Brain: Transmits set points to the *Controller* and monitors feedback values from the Controller.

2. Controller: Compares and calculates differences between the *Brain* set point value and *Feedback Device* current value. The signal created is called an error signal which is transmitted to the Amplifier (AMP).

3. Amplifier: Amplifies the *Controller* error signals to drive the *Motor* (if necessary) in the direction to achieve the set point.

4. Motor: Drives or manipulates the *Load* to achieve the desired set point.

5. Load: Is anything that will be manipulated. It could be air or a physical object.

6. Feedback Device: Sensing device that detects changes to the *Load.* It transmits a feedback signal to the *Controller* of the *Load* position (encoders, thermometer, pressure sensors, etc.).

Error Signal Theory:

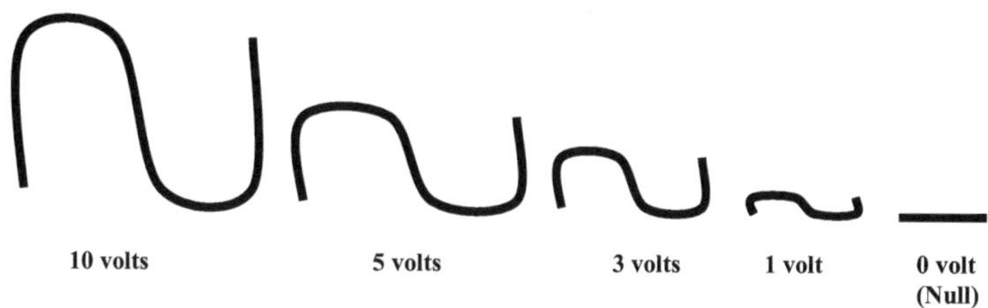

Diagram 1-3

The *Error Signal* or voltage is in proportion to the calculated difference between the *Brain* and the *Feedback Device.* The error signal decreases as the Load continues to get closer to the desired position.

For example:

Set Point = 30
Current Position = 20

Error Signal = **Set Point** - **Current Position** (30 - 20 = 10)

When the current position reaches 30, the system will be at the null state again.

Set Point = 30
Current Position = 30

Error Signal = 0 or Null (30 - 30 = 0)

FYI: *I estimate that approximately 85% of all equipment systems that I have worked on were designed using some variation of a basic closed-loop system. My understanding of this system has enabled me to manage various equipment platforms throughout my career.*

As you may have gathered, there is more to properly defining a problem than once thought. It does not take a *rocket-scientist* to determine that something is not working correctly. However, it does take time to try to comprehend how something works, how to structure your problem team, and how to evaluate the business impacts of the problem. Your problem team should contain the key stakeholders of your organization.

Summary: Phase 1 Problem Recognition

- Conduct a thorough business impact analysis of the problem.

- Determine the sense of urgency of your problem.

- Conduct a skills assessment and assemble your team.

- Identify a *problem-owner*. This individual will be responsible for fully comprehending all the variables and potential impacts involving this problem.

- Take the time required to ensure that you have properly defined the problem. A poorly defined problem will usually lead your team down endless rabbit trails.

- It is extremely important to ensure that your team will begin the process to solve an agreed upon problem. *High agreement* will enable you to focus your combined energy in the right direction.

- Ensure that you fully understand how the system functions before you began an aggressive troubleshooting effort. Use all available documentation and resources to improve your understanding.

I will use the following scenario throughout this book to help reinforce each phase of this process.

Practice Problem (True Story) - Gas heating system

Problem background: While living in beautiful Colorado Springs, Colorado, we heard a terrible sound from our gas heating system about 2:00 am. It sounded like a dying moose. Fortunately, it occurred before the winter months.

Problem Statement: The heating system is not maintaining the desired temperature.

Business Impact: *Decision time* – Because the Colorado winter was not in full swing, I decided to take on this challenge. A standard visit from a service technician, including labor was estimated at $2,000. My only obstacle was that I did not fully comprehend how a gas heating system operated.

Problem Description: A home heating system is designed to keep an area heated to a desired set point usually controlled by a thermostat. I began to study the system to better understand how it was designed to operate. I actually found a very simple wiring diagram that was attached to the panel of the heater unit along with some safety caution stickers. From this basic information I was able to comprehend how this system was actually designed to operate and all its safety precautions.

Gas Heating System Theory of Operation

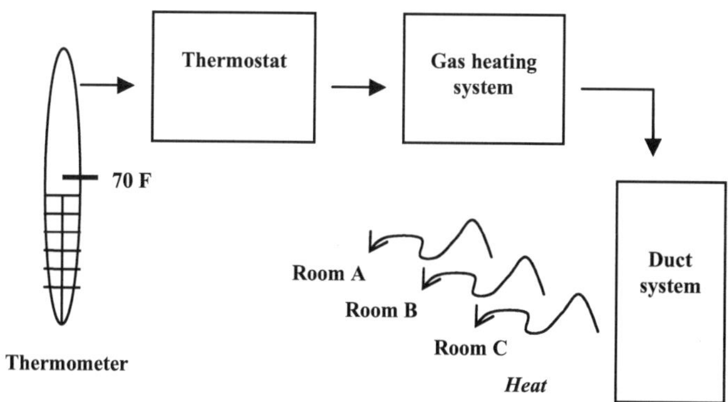

Diagram 1-4

1. **Thermometer** - measures temperature of the environment and transmits to the *Thermostat.*

2. **Thermostat** - regulates the temperature of the environment. Desired temperature setting is entered by the user and compared to the current temperature. If desired temperature is greater than current temperature, a signal is sent to the gas heating system.

3. **Gas heating system** - safely produces and forces gas-flamed heat into the duct system.

4. **Duct system** - transfers flame heat throughout the home.

Heating Unit Block

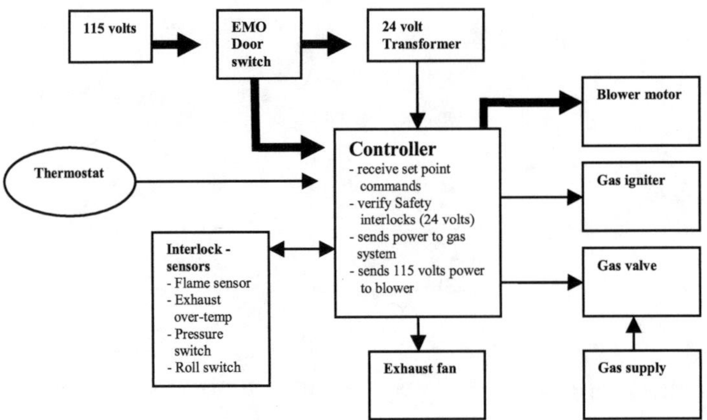

Diagram 1-5

Process Flow Description

1. When the *Thermostat* (mercury) set point is out of range, a 24 volt signal is sent to the *Controller* that begins the heating process.

2. The *Controller* ensures that all the safety features are not compromised (such as doors and over-temp switches). An open door will actually remove 115 volts from the circuit thus preventing the sequence to be completed. If a *sensor* or *interlock* is compromised, the system will shut down.

3. If no sensor compromise is detected, the *Exhaust Fan* will be energized with 115 volts.

4. The *Controller* checks the pressure switch that is attached to the *Exhaust Fan* to ensure that the exhaust fan is operating.

5. If no *sensor* or *interlocks* are compromised, the *Controller* will then send 24 volts to energize the *Gas Igniter* (burner).

6. The *Controller* sends 24 volts to the *Gas Valve* to allow gas to flow into the *Gas Igniter* to convert the gas into a flame.

7. The *Controller* senses a signal from the *flame sensor* that a flame is present.

8. The *Controller* sends 115 volts to the *Blower Motor* to force hot air throughout the *ventilation ducts*.

9. The *Controller* checks the over-temp limit switch to ensure the blower has turned on and is actually forcing the flamed heated air throughout the duct system. If an over-temp condition is sensed due to a faulty blower circuit, the system will shut down.

10. Once the desired temperature has been achieved, the thermostat will remove the 24 volts from the *Controller* to stop the process. The blower will usually remain on for a set amount of time to ensure that all the heated air is evacuated from the air duct system.

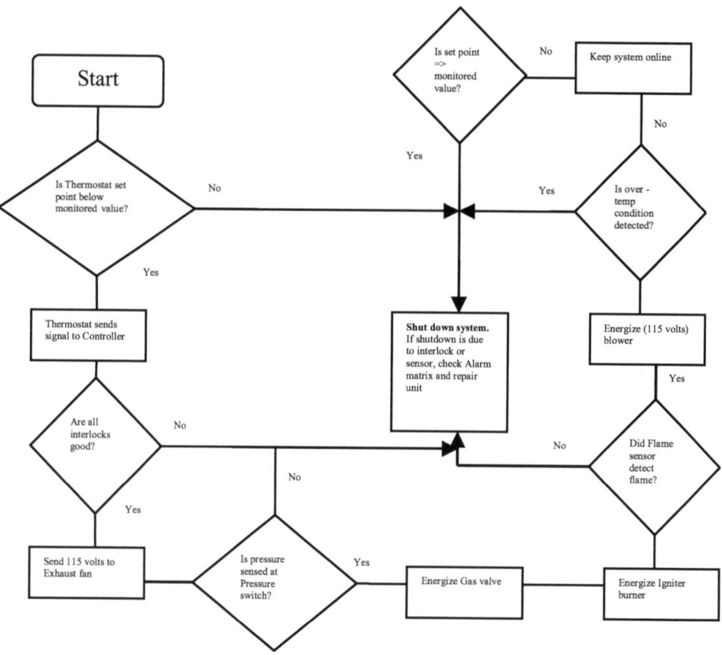

Process Flow Chart 1-1

Status Light (LED)	Equipment Problem	Check
On	Normal operation	-
One Blink	Ignition failure	• Gas flow • Gas pressure • Gas valve • Flame sensor
Two Blinks	Closed pressure switch	• Pressure switch failure • Bad connection
Three Blinks	Pressure switch failed to close	• Exhaust fan not energized • Pressure switch • Vent blockage
Four Blinks	Open over-temp limit switch	• Over-temp switch is opened • Over-temp is detected • Vent blockage
Five Blinks	False flame sensed	• Sticking gas valve • Faulty sensor
Rapid Continuous Blinking	Incorrect primary polarity	• Reversed transformer secondary • Reversed primary wires

Alarm Indicator Matrix Table 1-1

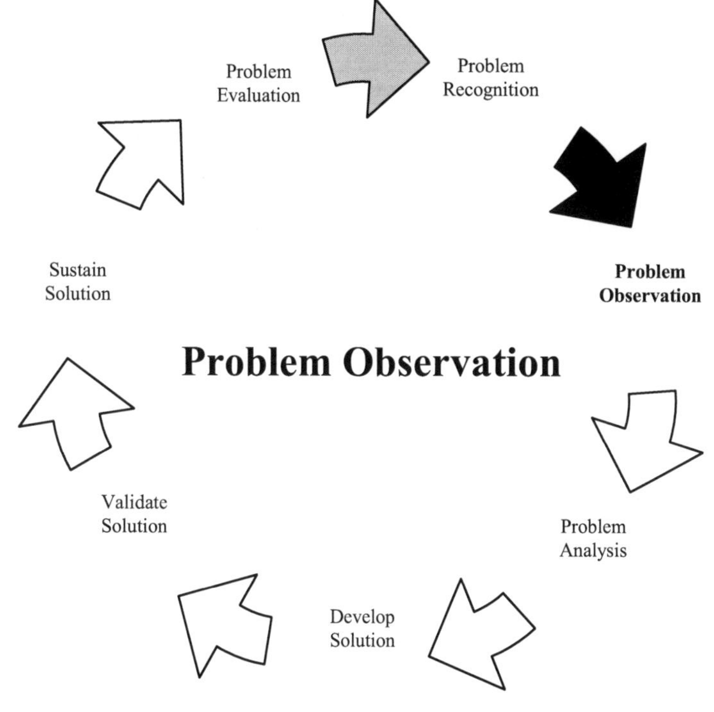
Problem
Evaluation
Problem
Recognition
Sustain
Solution
Problem
Observation
Problem Observation
Validate
Solution
Problem
Analysis
Develop
Solution

Chapter 3

Problem Observation

A reason some people fail and others succeed is their attention to detail.
- Edwin Lewis Cole

Professional problem-solvers such as detectives and forensic experts rely on their keen ability to carefully analyze and process crime scenes. They search for overlooked clues to aid them in solving some of the most difficult criminal cases. During the *Problem Recognition* phase, you comprehended your business impacts, assembled your team, developed a valid problem statement and obtained a thorough understanding of the system and process flow. Now you are ready to embark upon the next phase of the problem-solving process: *Problem Observation.*

During the *Problem Observation* phase, the primary goal of the problem-solver is to accurately characterize the nature of the problem as it presently exists. Oftentimes, many inexperienced problem-solvers are too quick to dive head first into a problem without carefully considering all the available information. As a result, existing problems can be overlooked, or worse yet, new problems could be induced due to improper or misinformed troubleshooting.

Moving fast is the not the same as going anywhere.
- Edwin Lewis Cole

Is the system in a *safe-state*?

Never assume that a system is safe to begin troubleshooting until you have verified and taken the appropriate actions to secure all forms of hazardous energy. Throughout my technical career this has been one area where I would absolutely trust no one, including myself. I double and triple check myself all the time to ensure that nothing has changed since my last encounter with a system. *You own your own safety!*

Have you conducted a *safety assessment* of the system?

Often, inexperienced problem-solvers are too quick to launch into a problem. In the process, they neglect to conduct a safety assessment of the equipment condition resulting in further system damage or worse: injury. The Bureau of Labor Statistics reported that in 2005 there were 394 fatalities in the manufacturing sector. (Bureau of Labor, 2005) Hazardous energy could cause further harm to people and equipment. The following is a list and examples of some of the most common hazardous energies:

- **Electrical** - Power, batteries and electronic components such as capacitors
- **Mechanical** - Gears, robotics and pinch-points
- **Thermal** - Chemical, heaters, radiation (RF) and cryogenics
- **Potential** - Hydraulic and pneumatics
- **Magnetic** - Powerful magnets can cause harm to pacemakers
- **Gas** - Toxics and corrosives

Before you begin to develop a troubleshooting strategy, ensure that you can place the equipment or system in a *safe-state*. Comprehend all of the potential hazards that are present. It could be as simple as locking out a circuit breaker or pulling out the power cord to ensure that the system cannot be energized or operated during your problem-solving.

For example: If you are an IT professional working with sensitive banking information, a *safe-state* to your profession could imply properly safe-guarding the customer's sensitive information prior to working on a server.

Only the Paranoid will Survive.
- Andy Grove
Former CEO

What available information do you have to substantiate this problem?

- **Equipment event logs** - Most advanced equipment contains an automated system log that tracks all alarms that have been generated to aid technicians during a troubleshooting effort. This valuable tool provides useful data to determine when and what alarms have occurred, which is extremely useful when you are developing a timeline.

- **Historical timeline** - A historical timeline is a great way to determine the chronological path of a problem. An accurately developed timeline can pinpoint when and what conditions contributed to the problem. Recent studies indicate that 70% of all problems are self-induced. Most timelines that I have developed usually correlate to a recent maintenance or activity that had occurred. An accurate timeline will uncover other hidden problems.

- **System failure timeline** - A system failure timeline is a great way to predict how long it will take before a system fails. This is a valuable tool if you have a current baseline. For example, if you are familiar with how long it takes for your car to start, you can immediately begin to detect when your battery may be becoming weak.

- **Eye-witness accounts -** If there were people around when the problem occurred, ask them to explain or describe any unusual conditions that existed.

- **Visual inspection -** Sparks, smoke or excessive motions. For example, sparks will usually indicate that you have an electrical problem which also indicates that your problem is not safe to evaluate until you have properly isolated the hazard. The experienced problem-solver will conduct a thorough visual inspection, looking at any unsafe conditions such as:

    - *Frayed electrical wires* - electrical hazard.
    - *Signs of overheating* - brittle wires or discolored insulation (brownish).
    - *Metal shavings around gears and bearings* - worn or binding mechanical components will usually begin to shed metal shavings of some sort.

- **Smells -** Some chemicals such as chlorine have a unique odor (swimming pool). Burning electrical and electronic components also exhibit distinctive odors.

- **Abnormal sounds -** Most mechanical failures are usually preceded by abnormal sounds. If possible, take the time to baseline the normal sounds of a piece of equipment. Every sound should have a corresponding action. As a technician, I was able to properly diagnose failing components based upon the type of sound that was observed during normal operations.

- **Statistical control charts -** Another excellent source of data. If properly analyzed, trends and shifts can be correlated to possibly explain other events in your timeline. *The Data Don't Lie.*

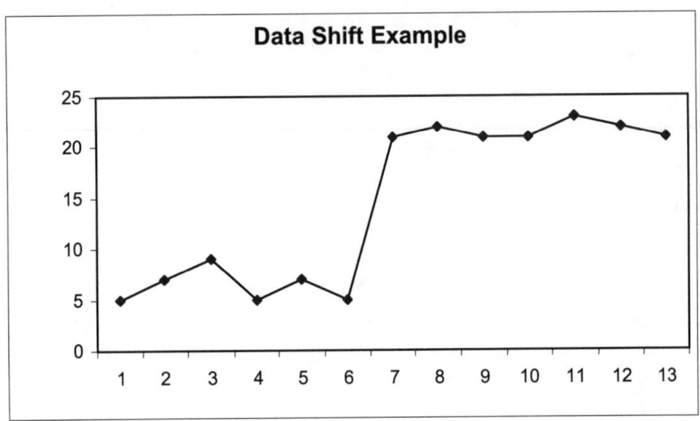

Data Shift Chart 3-1

A **data shift** is a clear indication that something went awry in your process. This is a classic example of how data will appear after a maintenance activity. Usually a wrong or marginal part has been introduced into the tool or a system is not properly calibrated.

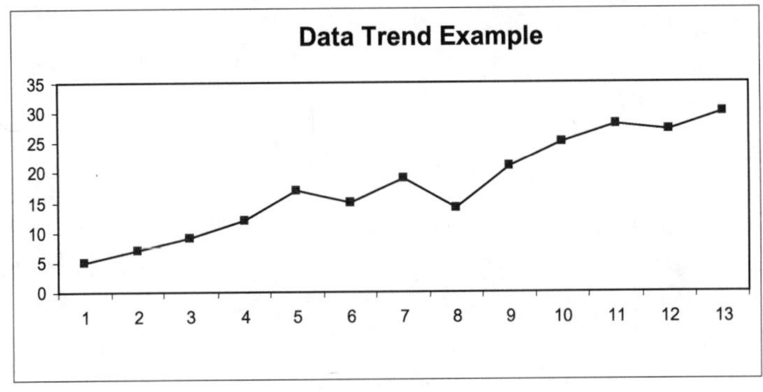

Data Trend Chart 3-2

A **trend** in data is usually an indication of a part or system degradation. Usually the troubleshooting effort leads to part replacement or calibration.

- **Equipment maintenance logs** - Per ISO (International Standards Organization) 9000 guidelines, companies are required to have adequate documentation systems in place. From my experience, automated systems are preferred. Technicians and engineers are required to annotate all maintenance activities that occur on a piece of equipment. This valuable information can be later retrieved from a database as needed to understand all actions that occurred chronologically to successfully develop an accurate timeline.

What system will be impacted by this problem?

In other words, what system is being implicated by the failure? Most advanced equipment contains multiple systems and sub-systems to achieve its primary objectives. For example, an automobile contains many systems that are required to function correctly so that you can drive safely.

- **Electrical system** - provides the necessary power to get the engine started.
    - *Battery*
    - *Alternator*
    - *Cables*
    - *Electronic modules*
    - *Starter*
    - *Distributor*
    - *Spark Plugs*
    - *Fuel Pump*

- **Mechanical system** - provides the necessary actions to move the vehicle.

    - *Transmission*
    - *Lubricants*
    - *Pistons*
    - *Starter*
    - *Brakes - pads*
    - *Hydraulics - such as brakes and steering components*

Most advanced equipment systems that I have maintained are usually designed to have some variations of a system failure indicator that can be easily deciphered.

- **LEDs (**light emitting diodes) - enable you to compare LED sequences to predetermined patterns to detect equipment failures.

- **Blinking LEDs** - are also commonly used in electrical household appliances such as heating systems in which a sequence of blinks corresponds to specific failures.

- **Automated alarm logs** - include descriptions that are used in your most advanced equipment configurations. These alarms not only alert you to what systems are affected, they also give you some helpful hints of possible problems.

*** ***CAUTION*** ***

Failure detection systems are not always accurate because they normally indicate only a ***manifestation*** *of a problem. I have also experienced failures in which the failure detection system was the problem because it was indicating erroneous failures.*

It is at this time that accurate data collection becomes extremely important. Some symptoms that may be observed will not always be associated with current failures, thus becoming ***A*** problem to be later addressed. Stay true to the data. Remember that ***The Data Don't Lie***. Be true to the data, and the data will be true to you during your analysis.

True Story: Load power failure

This was a very unique problem that eluded everyone. All indications pointed to the CPU (Central Processing Unit) or corrupted system software. The system would not properly complete its boot-up sequence. Like most problems, all the obvious components were replaced with no success. After conducting a timeline of the failure, I observed that this was a predictable failure. I noticed that when the motors for the transport system began to initialize, the system software would mysteriously shut down during the same timeframe (~50 seconds into the boot-up sequence). I decided to isolate the power to the servo motors to reduce the load on the affected power supply. To my amazement, the system software completed its boot-up sequence. I theorized that I was experiencing a ***load imbalance condition on the affected power supply****. I carefully began to energize each motor circuit until I was able to repeat the initial symptom. The root-cause of the problem was due to an aging power supply that was unable to support its current load rating.*

What is the frequency of the failure?

All failures are not the same. An experienced problem-solver should invest the time to properly understand the *frequency of the failure*. Simply put: how predictable is this failure? Based upon my experience I have concluded that the frequency of a failure falls into one of three categories or modes: ***Constant, Intermittent or Conditional.***

- ***Constant failures*** are easy to identify because the system does not operate any more (i.e. *it's no-worky*). This is usually an indication of a major component failure that is often easy to identify. For example, an attempt to start your car results in nothing. You later identify the failed component to be a battery that is fully drained. Constant failures can also be elusive especially if a wrong part is installed unknowingly.

- ***Intermittent failures*** are slightly complicated to categorize due to the nature or characteristics of the failure. They are difficult to predict, thus the hardest to truly solve. If the problem is not properly characterized or profiled, it could be very deceiving. Usually intermittent failures are a result of loose electrical connections or faulty wiring harnesses that have been damaged during a maintenance activity. Built-in-detection systems are usually deceived during these incidents. Pay close attention to these types of failures to determine what modulates the problem.

- ***Conditional failures*** are difficult problems to profile. They are similar to intermittent failures with the exception that it is possible to predict when the problem or failure will occur. These failures are usually symptoms of partially degraded components. Intermittent failures usually evolve into conditional failures when more information is discovered.

  Conditional failure examples:

  - *Range failures* are conditional failures in which components usually operate within a certain range. If the defined range is exceeded, the system will fail or perform erratically. For example, a Mass Flow Controller (MFC) is a gas distribution device that is designed to regulate gas flow over a specific range. The device may work fine at a lower range; however, it may not operate effectively at a higher range. In other words, if we are observing a device that will operate within a scale from 0 - 500, the device may operate correctly between 0 - 250, but begin to fail at gas flows greater than 300.

- *Temperature failures* are conditional failures usually caused by the failure of temperature controlled system components such as a faulty fan, liquid cooling system, heater, sensor or controller. The overall purpose of the temperature control system is to regulate the temperature of various systems for optimum performance. For example, a cooling fan's purpose is to simply dissipate heat from electronic devices so that the system can operate at an optimal temperature. If the fan fails, the system may operate normally for the initial hours of operation. However, if the system is allowed to continue to operate it will later begin to exhibit abnormal performance due to its inability to dissipate the heat.

True Story: Dirty Fuse Jack

During my early years in the high-tech manufacturing industry, I experienced a difficult hard-drive system failure. The system would mysteriously have hard-drive ***read/write*** *alarms. The hard-drive and all its associated parts were replaced numerous times per the alarms and the equipment manual recommendations. However, the system was experiencing the same intermittent problem. I decided to think out-of-the-box and go beyond the textbook recommendations and monitor all power inputs into the hard-drive controller system. To my surprise, I observed a floating 5 volts indication ranging from 4-5 volts. After carefully monitoring the voltage level with a digital volt meter, I made an awesome observation. When the voltage level dropped below 4.3 volts the hard-drive system would begin to have read/write alarms. Without interfering with the system the voltage would begin to increase again.*

After comparing my results to a ***known-good*** *system, I also observed that the voltage was steady at 5 volts without any variation. After this observation, I began to trace the physical wiring connections in which I later discovered that the problem was directly associated with a* ***dirty fuse jack.*** *The fuse jack had oxidation build-up that was preventing a proper connection for the fuse. This problem had plagued our team for months. During a thorough problem evaluation, this problem was later traced to a previous problem that had been* ***fixed*** *but not properly* ***solved****.*

FYI: *When possible, compare suspected bad systems to a* ***known-good*** *system as a reference. This is also referred to as fingerprinting or equipment-matching.*

Check-Point #1

Scenario	Constant	Intermittent	Conditional
The lawn mower will not start.	X		
I noticed that after 5 minutes into my shower that the hot water became lukewarm. However, I also noticed that after it was idled for approximately an hour it was hot again.			X
Sometimes my car starts immediately without hesitation while other times it stalls for about 10 seconds or so.		X	
The robot will not move when I give it a command signal.	X		
The gas is not flowing when the gas valve solenoid is activated.	X		
Sometimes the gas flows while other times nothing happens when the gas solenoid valve is activated.		X	
Every time it rains I notice my internet connection becomes erratic.			X

Frequency Failure Table 2-1

Annotate all findings. Document... Document!

Writing down information is a great way of tracking your progress. It is also extremely helpful during the later phases, and facilitates proper pass-downs to other technicians during shift changes. Document even the most trivial observations; they will be critical when you begin to analyze all your data. Keep a notebook handy to capture your ideas as you contemplate your findings.

Unfortunately, many of today's technical professionals do not fully comprehend the value of properly documenting and sharing their work. They usually think it is a waste of time that distracts from ***real troubleshooting***. They fail to recognize the art of documenting as a vital component of troubleshooting. The documentation can be later used to develop *Best Known Methods* (BKMs) or new specification changes. In the event the person cannot continue supporting the problem, the documentation provides a roadmap for the team to pursue. The documentation should contain the current problem statement and description. It should have a list of all the theories that have been explored and the actions that have been taken. Intuitively, I can discern how effective a problem-solving effort is by how much documentation is available to support the effort. Teams that do not value accurate documentation usually become the victims of *shot-gunning, easter-egging, and swaptronics approaches.*

Good documentation examples:

- Technical Manuals
- Presentations
- System diagrams and schematics
- A list of the current ***A*** problems that were uncovered
- A precise list of all actions taken and current plan
- A list of theories that have been explored
- A historical time-line of the problem
- Equipment alarms logs

- Frequency of failure category (*Constant, Intermittent, or Conditional*)
- Statistical data to support problems to determine trends or shifts
- Business impact
- Boundary conditions

True Story: Up the River without a Paddle

During one of my many deployments in the Navy, I vividly recall being literally stuck at the mouth of the Willamette River without a working gyrocompass navigation system. We pulled into a small town at the mouth of the river to pick up some passengers on our way to the Annual Fleet Day festival in Portland, Oregon. During our brief overnight visit, one of the two gyrocompass systems failed.

FYI: *Trying to navigate a naval warship up a twisting, turbulent river without a gyrocompass is not a good idea.*

Well, one of my peers decided to save the day in the middle of the night by taking down the only good gyrocompass system to remove a component to prove his theory. Needless to say, he did not ask for permission nor did he seek my advice regarding his decision. To his surprise, he also damaged the known good component. When our commanding officer heard about this... let's just say it was not a good day. After further investigation, we discovered that a connector-pin in the card slot that housed the circuit card of the faulty system was actually penetrating through the circuit card into one of its components. This caused a short circuit.

As a result, we were late to the festival. The commanding officer asked all of our distinguished guests to depart the boat. We had to have the supplier fly in a part to enable us to safely navigate the river. I still wonder what happened to that guy.

Modify your problem statement.

Look at the problem statement and remain on track. Modify your problem statement as you get more insightful information regarding your problem. This new information may require you to revisit your previous assumptions. For example, you could have a problem that is characterized as an ***intermittent*** problem that could be easily re-characterized as a ***conditional*** problem as you uncover more pertinent information. Understanding the frequency of the failure will help you identify probable causes more accurately. The mark of a good problem-solver is their ability to continue to adjust their problem statement with the data they uncover. Often you can identify feasible options to enable your system to operate at a reduced capacity that may buy you some time to meet temporary objectives. Other times, you may determine a major flaw in your original problem statement, which will enable you to declare the system *un-safe* to operate.

True Story: Attention to Detail

During my early years as a technician, I was assigned to solve a very difficult problem. The system failure was manifested as a mechanical failure. Previous technicians had conducted several major rebuilds of this system to only induce other problems. We eventually returned to the original problem... thus the quote:

Moving fast does not mean that you are going anywhere.
- Edwin Lewis Cole

After realizing that this was a very unusual problem, I decided to approach it with much caution. I decided to conduct a very thorough observation of the problem to attempt to characterize the nature of the failure. The system operated flawlessly ***without any indications of mechanical binding*** *in which the generated error code was specifically indicating. However* *after conducting a system failure timeline of the problem, I observed that the problem would occur* ***within the first hour.*** *I also observed that there was no mechanical binding that could have caused the alarm. As I cleared the alarm to continue my test, the failures would occur* ***more frequently*** *until it could be repeated* ***every two minutes****. I then allowed the system to remain idle for about two hours while I contemplated the failure during a break. After regrouping, I returned to repeat the test again only to get the same results. I successfully created the* ***fail condition*** *that was repeatable and predictable. I theorized that this problem was temperature related because the problem was modulated with time. The two-hour delay enabled the system to dissipate heat. I later went on to discover that one of the two cooling fans that were used to dissipate heat in the electronic enclosure had failed due to faulty bearings.*

FYI: *Degrading mechanical components don't mysteriously repair themselves.*

The overheating of the electronic enclosure unit was causing a condition known as ***thermal runaway*** *within the semiconductor components on the circuit board. The condition was causing erroneous alarms due to excessive heat.*

True Story: Bad Team Problem-Solving

I wish I could say that the story ended there, but it didn't. The part that was needed was not available on-site. I placed an order for the part, and was told the part may arrive in 48hrs. However, I was able to locate an electrically compatible fan that could be installed. I communicated to the on-coming shift precisely what was required to complete the repair until the new part arrived as a ***temporary containment strategy****. I also instructed my peers to ensure the fan was installed in the correct position so that it would be removing air from the enclosure and not blowing hot air into the unit. To my surprise* *and dismay, my peer technician had begun another major rebuild and during the process had once again* ***induced another problem*** *by damaging a hard-to-get part. I was stunned by his actions. I presented my concerns to my then engineering team who directed me to a system from which I could retrieve the part that was damaged. Upon completing the repair, I inspected the work that I had instructed the individual to perform only to discover that the fan was indeed* ***installed in the wrong direction.*** *By this time the correct part had arrived. I then installed the correct fan assembly and the system passed my initial test* ***by not failing within the first hour of operation****.*

I wish I could say the story ended... but it didn't. *The technician was in such disbelief of my analysis of the problem, that he later removed the assembly that I installed to test my theory. To his astonishment, the very symptom returned just as I had predicted. As we used to say as children in the south –* ***If I'm lying, I'm flying.***

I also wish I could say that this was a rare occasion, but it wasn't. Earlier during my technical career this happened more often than I would like to admit, but I will get into team relationship problems later on in the book.

Summary: Phase 2 Problem Observation

- If at all possible or plausible, attempt to safely recreate the problem condition. Some problems cannot be recreated safely; appropriate actions should be taken to place the equipment in a *safe-state.*

- Collect and review all relevant equipment history logs, documents, and charts associated with the problem. Most technical and owner's manuals such as a Chilton automotive manual will have a *theory of operation* section describing in simple terms how the system operates.

- Develop an accurate historical and system failure timeline.

- Characterize the problem – *constant, intermittent, or conditional.*

- Conduct a thorough visual inspection of the system; look for any anomalies.

- Properly document all your discoveries and observations even if they seem trivial.

- Keep reviewing your problem statement and remain on track.

- Double check your data for accuracy and false assumptions.

- Modify your problem statement.

Back to our gas heating system problem...

Problem Statement: The gas heating system is not maintaining the desired temperature.

Problem Background: Winter has not yet begun. Funds are limited. Husband is willing and has time to work on the problem.

Problem Observations:

1. The gas heating system is making a loud disturbing noise; like a sick moose.

2. The blower will intermittently run ~ 2 hours before rapidly winding down to a halt. The blower began to make a loud hum before eventually shutting off.

3. The blower shaft can be turned by hand - no excessive binding was observed.

4. Blower was covered in dust.

5. Air Filter was dirty.

6. All electrical connections were verified per the electrical schematic attached to the panel; no discoloration, frayed or exposed wires were observed.

7. All metering checks were good throughout the interlock sensors.

8. The gas ignition system was producing a sustainable flame.

9. Once the blower stopped and began to hum, the flame/gas would remain on for about 10 minutes before the system would shut-down.

10. After allowing the system to cool, it would sometimes start back up before eventually rotating rapidly to a halt. Sometimes the blower would simply begin making a loud humming sound.

11. I noticed after the system shutdown, I was getting a series of blinking lights on the *Controller* (four blinking lights).

12. An attached alarm matrix on the panel door indicated that the *over-temp switch* is faulty or an actual over-temp condition has been detected.

13. The last failure was due to a faulty over-temp switch (covered under warranty) two years ago.

14. The furnace has been in service for five years.

15. I found a loose electrical wire that was not connected.

16. Current system configuration was programmed to allow the blower to operate continuously.

17. System documentation was poor; only a basic component wiring diagram and alarm matrix was available on the panel.

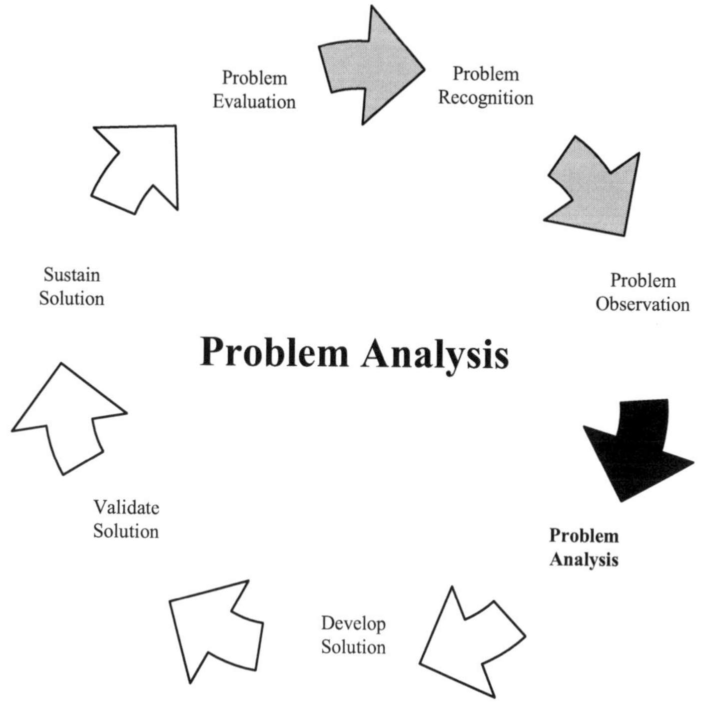
Problem
Evaluation
Problem
Recognition
Problem
Observation
Sustain
Solution
Problem Analysis
Problem
Analysis
Validate
Solution
Develop
Solution

Chapter 4

Problem Analysis

Failure is not an option.
– Apollo 13

Congratulations!!! You are now ready to begin the most difficult part of problem-solving, especially when working in a team environment. Now you have to ask yourself, *what does all of this mean?* This is also the phase where most effective problem-solving begins to collapse. During heated discussions, usually members of your team sprout egos as they begin to feel threatened if their ideas are challenged or their interpretation of the data is questioned. Remember all ideas are correct until accurately proven wrong. High agreement is extremely important during this phase of the process. A *disagree-and-commit* strategy is not desirable... let the data, not opinions primarily lead the problem-solving effort. The pressure from management to solve the problem will often times exacerbate the situation. Your strong facilitation skills as a leader are paramount to enable your team to avoid the pitfalls of a stalemate. During *Problem Analysis* phase of the process you will learn: how to effectively facilitate problems in a team environment, strategies to identify and address team member problems and how to accurately analyze your data.

In God we trust, all others must bring data.
- Dr. W. Edwards Deming

Changing the Atmosphere

During the data analysis phase I have found it better to take the team into a conference room away from the problem and from anxious managers who are very interested in the progression of the problem-solving effort. Location is extremely important to solving problems. A conference room allows everyone to speak freely regarding the problem at hand. As the problem-owner, you should set the tone of the meeting so everyone can freely share their ideas. No one should be able to hide behind titles or positional authority. *Failure is not an option.* The problem-owner must establish an environment for innovative ideas to be unleashed among the team. Nothing is impossible. Never assume. No rock is left unturned. As they say in Vegas… *what happens in Vegas, stays in Vegas.* Re-establish ground rules if necessary to ensure your meeting's success. These meetings can become very stimulating as the team begins to collectively analyze the data. Be prepared for healthy tension among the team.

Can't Died with Won't

Growing up in the south I recall my grandmother always saying this phrase. Basically, the phrase means that if you say that you ***can't*** *do something, you have not tried hard enough. If you say you* ***won't*** *do something, you are rebelling and stubborn. Both of these statements are unacceptable, therefore…* ***Can't Died with Won't.***

Never under estimate the value of a good-nights sleep

Fatigue destroys innovative thinking. Exhaustion usually fuels heated debates among your team members. Fatigue is at the origin of most hasty decisions. Make sure you and your team are getting enough rest to promote creative thinking. Many times, I have pulled the plug on brainstorming sessions and other activities because the team was simply too mentally exhausted to effectively continue. Occasionally, to promote my creative thinking abilities, I would simply sleep-in a few extra hours in the morning prior to going to work. I also make an attempt to engage in a exercise program to enable me to escape from the problem at hand to clear my mind. As the problem-owner, you should be constantly aware of your team's ability to perform in a high stress environment. Fatigue usually precedes safety incidents and opportunity loss. Colin Powell, the former U.S. Secretary of State and Joint Chief of Staff, says that when possible he tries to avoid making decisions until all the data has been properly evaluated. Patience usually enables you to make a more informed decision.

True Story: Frustrated Problem Team – With All the Answers

During one occasion, I was asked to facilitate a problem that one of our teams was experiencing. The problem was relatively straight-forward; however, the team was so frustrated with one another that no one was actually listening. They were simply going in circles chasing their tails. Team members were arguing openly over their cubicles. The technicians were fed up with doing useless time-wasting experiments to appear to be busy. The tension was so apparent that you could have cut it with a knife. As a leader on my team, I decided to step in to facilitate the problem because the problem team had ***become... A*** *problem. I asked the new engineer and a senior technician who were passionately disagreeing with the current plan to present their reasons for disagreeing with the plan. To their combined surprise, I agreed with their positions after carefully evaluating all their data. The junior engineer had collected all the data surrounding the problem that accurately revealed a much greater problem than they once thought.*

Her frustration was due to the fact that she was fresh out of college, new to the team, and no one respected her position. Another contributing factor was that there was no clear ownership of the problem. The senior technician apologized to the new engineer multiple times during the meeting because she truly held the key information to really understanding the problem. After a four-hour meeting on a Friday afternoon, we were able to accurately characterize the problem and formulate a strategy to address the root-cause. I was able to involve everyone in the solution so that they could have a sense of ownership.

I'm proud to report that the system was up within 12 hours after it had been down for five days of futile troubleshooting attempts. As a result, the problem team was able to understand why it is essential to have high agreement. Our solution was later adopted by others as a permanent solution to an age-old problem. One of the secrets that I have learned is to...

Do everything; take credit for nothing.

What do you do when your Team becomes a part of the problem?

I'm often asked this question when I'm speaking to various groups of professionals. I think the question alone deserves a dedicated section if not a book and/or a workshop. As problem-team leaders, you will be challenged to work with difficult team members who may attempt to derail your efforts if ignored. I have tried various strategies throughout my career to mitigate these complicated issues; some were successful and others were not. I would like to believe that everyone on the problem team is there because they have a vested interest and a high level of passion to solve the problem; not to simply fix the problem or to protect their interest. Here is my strategy when I find myself in this situation:

> *Opinions are like feet; most everyone has one or two and they usually stink.*
>
> **– Doug Stuhr**
> *US Navy Retired*

- **Value people's opinions** - Don't invest too much energy debating everyone's opinion. I have learned that some people love to hear themselves talk even if they are saying nothing of value. As the problem-team leader, I effectively capture their thoughts in writing. This can be achieved by using a whiteboard or a notepad. Restating what was said is also an effective technique. Both techniques enable me to gather everyone's input in a timely fashion. It is important to engage all of the team members early; failure to do so can potentially derail your problem-solving efforts.

- **Get high agreement** - Make sure that everyone is in high agreement of the problem and the proposed strategy to solve this problem. Failure to do so can and will cause a rift in your efforts.

- **Confront the issue** - Frequently an unwilling participant will not fully contribute to the efforts by concealing pertinent information from the team. If I sense this within my team, I will usually try to speak to the individual in private to fully understand his/her position. *Address the issue, not the individual.* Do not assume that person is trying to hinder the efforts. *Reward in public; discipline in private.*

- **Escalate issue** - If the individual continues to refuse to get on board with the rest of the team, I will usually make another effort to address the issue with the individual in an attempt to salvage the relationship. If the problem persists, I will usually bring it to the attention of my direct manager or the *manager-in-charge.*

- **Do not avoid the issue** - Avoiding the issue could jeopardize your ability to effectively solve the problem at hand. It can also destroy friendships. It will cause your company to lose profits due to missed opportunities. Don't allow intimidation to be a factor. Nor should you allow your personal relationships to interfere with your responsibility as the problem-team leader.

- **Salvage the relationship** - Always attempt to salvage the relationship if the individual is removed from the team. I try not to take it personally when I'm leading a problem-solving effort. High stress is a by-product of solving complex problems in a non-structured environment. I try to bring humor in the problem-solving efforts to diffuse the stress. Don't wait for a formal apology; it may never happen. Be the bigger person, take the high road; find the opportunity to defuse the tension over a cup of coffee.

Signs when your Problem-Team has become "A" Problem

- When your team is constantly arguing.
- When your team meetings almost end up in a fist fight.
- When you come around, people stop talking or leave.
- When members of your team are having a separate meeting during your meeting.
- When only certain members of your team are privileged to review important details.
- When your team members ask you…Why are you here?
- When members of your team confront you and tell you to stop trying to change things.
- When team members are not held accountable for their actions.
- When you walk pass a conference room only to discover that your team is having a meeting without you.

Beware of problem team member personalities

1. **Streakers** tend to be members of your team who enjoy being at the center of attention. They tend to jockey or compete for the leadership role of the team. However, when given the opportunity they usually fail to lead the team to any real resolution.

    - ***Recommended Strategy:*** *Attempt to involve them early in the problem. Assign them high visible tasks. When and if they fail to deliver the expected outcome, begin to gain their trust by offering your help in the matter. You should make every effort to harness their energy. Good leaders seek to develop other leaders.*

2. **Spin-Masters** tend to challenge every idea irregardless of the data; which is not necessarily bad. However, they rarely offer any real solutions of their own. *The glass is always half empty.* They are difficult to persuade and are usually overly cautious to buy-in or agree to the problem team's plans even with supporting data.

    - ***Recommended Strategy:*** *Smartly and **publicly** within the team, challenge the individuals to give reasons or supporting data for disagreeing with proposed theories and solutions. Solicit ideas from the individuals to be presented to the team for open discussion. Ensure that they have ample opportunity to provide supporting data for their positions.*

3. **Playa-Haters** are the team members who seemingly are always attacking the character of the leader or the other team members. They are usually at the origin of every malicious rumor or inappropriate comment. As we say in the south, they are always stirring up the pot for

trouble. They are usually guilty of misrepresenting the truth and violating the team's communication ground rules.

- ***Recommended Strategy**: **Privately** address your **primary** concerns with the individuals, but not necessarily the **specifics** to avoid adding fuel to the fire. Seek to understand why these individuals are **seemingly** resisting your efforts. Listen carefully to their response to determine how you can broker a deal to enlist their support. Establish some specific ground rules that you can adhere to. Immediately escalate the matter if the problem persists.*

4. **Silent-Storms** are the team members who are *unusually* silent during team meetings. They will not aggressively challenge ideas even if they perceive flaws in your assumptions. They are too quick to agree with whatever the team decides. Because they often feel as though no one values their input, as a defense mechanism they slowly disengage their efforts to silently protest. They have learned the art of *disagreeing and committing quickly* to allow the team to move forward.

    - ***Recommended Strategy: Privately** address your primary concerns with the individual. Listen carefully to their response to determine how you can remove barriers that have caused them to disengage. Re-assure them of their value to the team and follow-up accordingly with their concerns to regain their trust.*

5. **Lone-Rangers** are similar to the silent storms, except they **don't** disengage. They usually withhold information or ideas from the team. They privately

conduct their own test strategies to prove the team wrong. Unfortunately, their plans are usually not properly documented or analyzed by the team to determine its overall impact to the problem-solving effort. Their efforts usually result in wasted resources and time.

- ***Recommended Strategy**: Smartly and **publicly** solicit input from the individuals during team discussions. Ensure that they have ample opportunity to share information to the team for evaluation. Ensure that everyone in the meeting agrees to follow the proposed strategy without deviating. Establish a ground rule not to deviate from the plan without the problem-owner or team's consent. This strategy makes the individual accountable to the team and not you.*

6. **Used-Car Salesmen** are the *fast talkers* of the team. No one can seem to *get a word in edgewise.* They are usually fixated on one observation or solution irregardless of the overall data analysis. They are skillful at driving the team to quickly make assumptions and conclusions based upon *their* evaluation of the data. It is difficult to pin them down to exactly one statement or position. For example, in one statement they will state that $\boldsymbol{A + B = C}$. You, later conclude that if $\boldsymbol{A + B = C}$... then $\boldsymbol{B + A = C}$ based upon the rule of addition. They will passionately disagree with you by saying... *not exactly... it is complicated.* Unlike the *Spin Master*, they have a valid idea, but it just doesn't feel right... kind of like *buyer's remorse.* You know... that uneasy feeling you have after you make a spontaneous major purchase.

   - ***Recommended Strategy:** This could be a very sensitive situation. Oftentimes, the individual is trying to protect their personal interest by* *apparently **clouding** the information that the team has methodically compiled. Publicly and smartly, challenge the individual by trying to get them to settle on a position or theory. Continue to challenge them to demonstrate or **explain in simple terms** what they are recommending. In doing so, you may expose subtle motives and a lack of true overall system knowledge. You will also make them accountable to the team and not you. Oftentimes, they will usually quietly disappear from your team meetings to pursue other projects. It is your goal to slow them down so that the team can avoid making a hasty decision. Again, seek to understand why they appear to be in a hurry to quickly make a decision. I learned this strategy from the TV detective Colombo; he was the master at simplifying complicated and mysterious crimes.*

7. **Conspiracy-Theorists** are team members who are always implying some secretive undercover plot is going on. They normally get obsessed with one idea, solution or certain observation even though the overall data doesn't support their conclusion. They can get down-right spooky at times. It is like they are always trying to put a big circular peg in a small square hole; it just doesn't fit.

   - ***Recommended Strategy:*** *Celebrate their creativity; but keep them focused on the known information. Pay special attention to what they are saying. Many times they have great innovative ideas that only they can come up with because of their unique perspective. My favorite phrase to listen for is -* ***You know… the funny thing is… blah, blah, blah.*** *Oftentimes, a major piece to your problem-solving puzzle is embedded within this statement. These members keep the problem-solving effort humorous and adventurous. 95% of the time they may be* ***out-***

> ***to-lunch****, but 5% of the time they will unknowingly have a stroke of pure genius. Keep these members close to you so that they don't get discouraged by other members not respecting their creativity. They will usually keep you laughing.*

I have offered you some effective strategies that I routinely employ. However, you should develop your own unique strategies to compliment your personality and leadership style. Addressing issues in a timely manner will prevent the negative impacts that will be inflicted upon your problem-solving efforts. It is extremely important that the problem team leader recognize these and other disruptive personalities when they surface.

Seek to understand before assuming these individuals are simply trying to hinder the team's efforts or personally attack your character. Oftentimes you will uncover secondary issues such as family or other personal tragedies that are affecting their ability to adequately engage into the problem-solving efforts. No one on the team is immune from these personalities. Like many, I'm usually guilty of becoming a silent storm when I feel undervalued. I have also witnessed some schizophrenic team members who can exhibit multiple personalities in one meeting.

True Story: Sick and Tired of Being Sick and Tired.

I was assigned to work with a team that was struggling with their targeted objectives. This team was on the slippery slope to disaster. There was minimum cohesiveness among the team members. I was asked to support their effort. As an outsider playing the role of an internal consultant, I was immediately resisted by most of the team. A senior member of the team let it be known immediately that I was not welcomed. This individual exhibited various problem team personalities (schizophrenic) towards my efforts. It did not take too long before the individual publicly displayed their thoughts regarding my efforts within the team. Understanding the sensitivity of the situation, I allowed the individual to vent their frustration. To their amazement, I resisted the temptation to be drawn into verbal warfare. I later learned that the individual had a family member that was preparing to under-go a very risky operation. Privately, I talked to the individual regarding the situation and their open resistance of my efforts among the team. I encouraged the individual to be with their family. I explained to them that it was not my goal to demean their efforts. I indirectly negotiated a ground-rule to fully support their efforts to improve the team's overall performance. The individual later took time off work to tend to their family.

When the individual returned, their area was making a comeback. I smartly resisted the temptation to remain within the group and later returned to my original team. In hind site, I was glad that I did not take the initial burst of frustration personally. If my family member was in the hospital and my efforts to lead my area were being questioned, I would have been tempted to respond similarly.

In conclusion, knowing how to manage problem team members and various issues when they manifest will enable you to keep your problem-solving efforts on track. It is important to value everyone's opinion and to get high agreement to harness the synergy within your team. If a team member is not fully contributing; seek to understand why. Do not ignore the problem. Communicate the problem to your manager and seek to salvage the relationship. Now let's get back to the *Problem Analysis* phase.

Identify root-cause and containment strategies

Our goal during the *Problem Analysis* phase is to methodically analyze all the data that we observed and compiled. It is also important to identify all possible root-causes and containment strategies for our current problem. Identifying a *temporary containment strategy* can give you some leverage to negotiate alternatives that may satisfy your crucial business objectives. *Permanent containment strategies* will enable you to get your system back to its optimum state.

What is the nature or characteristic of the problem?

From my experience, I have surmised that equipment failures have specific characteristics that make them unique: *Mechanical, Electrical, Electronic, Temperature or Software.* For example, problems that are mechanical in nature have specific characteristics that are different from electrical and electronic problems such as a grinding noise. Also, each characteristic correlates to a unique failure frequency as we previously reviewed. Mechanical failures are easy to predict because most of the time you can visually or audibly observe the incident to determine the conditions surrounding the failure.

There are five natures of failures:

1. Mechanical
2. Electrical
3. Electronics
4. Temperature
5. Software/programming/configuration

Mechanical:

Frequency of failure - *Conditional/Constant.* Once failure begins, it will only get worse. Mechanical failures exhibit erratic operation. Binding gears produce grinding sounds, shed metal particles and oftentimes produce heat due to friction. Mechanical failures are most often a result of part degradation. Aging parts due to wear and tear will gradually become worse. All mechanical failures are not audible or visual. However, due to their unique characteristics they are easy to predict.

Examples:

- Motors are unusually warmer than normal. Current overloaded circuits will most likely trip due to the excessive heat caused by an increase in current flow.

- Motor shaft bearings will normally malfunction or seize up due to aging lubricant or normal degradation.

- Mechanical systems may operate normally; however, during extended repairs or maintenance activities these systems can become inoperative.

- Data trends are great indicators of degrading parts (wear-and-tear).

Electrical:

Frequency of failure - *Intermittent/Conditional.* These failures can be a result of a faulty cable harness, inadequate connections, or degraded parts.

- One of the greatest contributors to an electrical failure is a lack of *attention-to-detail* during maintenance activities. Wiring harnesses are usually not properly routed around moving parts such as motor shafts and gears. Electrical components are easily damaged during re-assembling.

Frequency of failure – *Constant.* These failures are due to broken or severed wires, wiring-harnesses or electrically opened circuits. For safety reasons circuits will open to prevent incidental operations.

Examples:

- **Emergency Machine Off (EMO)** - Designed to protect personnel from high voltage exposure such as 208 volts. If the switches are activated, the entire system will shut down.

- **Safety interlocks -** Designed to protect personnel from hazardous energy exposure such as radiation or gear systems. These interlocks are usually electrical switches or light sensor devices.

- **Overheating** - Frayed or brownish wire insulation are obvious signs of overheating which could be a result of a power load imbalance condition. Fuses are electrical devices that are designed to interrupt the flow of current in the event that a load draws too much current from the source.

Electronic:

Frequency of failure - *Intermittent/Conditional.* These failures are due to degrading components or overheating. Parts that are operating in a less than desired environment will eventually begin to exhibit unusual behaviors that are difficult to profile.

- For example, most electronic components are designed to operate in a cool environment to prevent *thermal runaway.* Thermal runaway is a condition that enables depletion regions of solid state devices to shrink, allowing electrons to flow due to excessive heat even though they are not properly biased.

Frequency of failure - *Constant.* These failures are due to damaged components caused by mishandling and/or part degradation.

- For example, electronic components and PCBs (Printed Circuit Boards) should remain in the ESD (Electro-Static Discharge) protected packaging until they are ready to be installed. Parts that are mishandled will be subject to vibration shock that can weaken poorly soldered components. Parts that are improperly removed from the ESD packaging can be easily exposed to static electricity generated by the handlers.

Software/programming/configuration:

Frequency of failure - *Constant/Conditional.* Most failures are due to improper settings.

Examples:

- An operating part inserted into a system that is not configured properly will continue to appear as a failing part until the program or software parameters are corrected.

- Oftentimes software parameters are accidentally altered (***fat-fingered)*** by individuals as they peruse screens during troubleshooting and maintenance efforts.

- Programs could also be attacked by malicious viruses.

- Printed circuit boards (PCBs) are manufactured to enable end-users to configure units for various operation modes. If the configuration settings are not properly verified, the PCB will only induce other problems.

Rule of thumb when replacing a PCB

Verify the configuration settings and revision numbers of the original PCB before installing a replacement PCB into a system. Do not discard the original PCB until the system is functioning correctly.

- **Software interlocks** - Designed to protect the equipment and personnel from improper operations. The software is programmed to monitor the system activity.

Temperature:

Frequency of failure – *Conditional.* Temperature failures are difficult to detect. These problems are usually manifested when the suspect system is allowed to operate for a certain period of **time** in an uncontrolled environment. Faulty cooling fans will not be able to effectively dissipate heat from electronics. In time, the system will overheat inducing premature wear and tear and thermal runaway.

Frequency of failure – *Constant.* Temperature control is extremely important in the high-tech manufacturing industry. Heaters or other heating devices are usually embedded in the equipment frames to enable a uniform temperature control. Oftentimes these heaters operate in groups. If one heater fails, you will experience a product uniformity problem. In other words... only that portion of the product is affected.

Check-Point #2

Scenario	Mechanical	Electrical	Temperature	Electronic	Software
During your observation you hear a grinding noise before the system alarms.	X				
Upon the completion of a maintenance activity you noticed that the RF power generator would only produce half the requested power when the set point is set for maximum power.				X	X
You noticed that the longer you allow your system to operate the more mysterious your indications are. Sometimes you get alarms that simply do not correlate with your observations.			X	X	
You observed that the system you are monitoring is having intermittent alarms that only occur when the mechanical components of the system are in motion. You also do not observe any signs of bindings (sounds or shavings).		X			

Failure Characteristics Table 3-1

What is the *Data* trying to tell you?

Based on your collected data and observations, begin to closely examine the true characteristics of the problems. Don't forget to consider all possibilities: e.g., degrading parts, broken wires, improper calibration, and unqualified individuals performing work etc. It is very possible to have multiple problems contributing to the same symptom. *Nothing is impossible.* Initially, avoid *over-analyzing* the problem. Remember; keep your *conspiracy theorist* close to you. Some major equipment problems require very simple repairs that require little effort, but great attention to detail. However, there will be times when you have to go beyond your collected data due to system and equipment limitations. The **data** may not agree with your problem observations.

For example, let's assume that your car actually ran out of fuel when your fuel meter was indicating that you had one-fourth tank of gas available. Your overall data analysis concluded that your gas indication meter is out of calibration or simply malfunctioning. Therefore, you can't rely on its ability to accurately indicate the amount of fuel that is available.

Use the KISS (Keep It Simple Stupid) principle

Avoid over-analyzing. This usually occurs as a result of TMI (Too Much Information), IO (Information Overload), (NEI) Not Enough Information, or a *conspiracy-theorist* gone wild. Oftentimes, egos begin to override wisdom and the facts on the table due to the seniority of certain members. Look for the simple solutions first.

Remember:

- A faulty cooling fan unit can cause electronic circuitry to give false signals due to thermal-runaway. Thermal-runaway is a process in which electrons tend to flow freely across junction barriers due to high temperatures.

- A *hard-drive* problem was the result of losing a 5 volt signal caused by a dirty fuse jack.

Stay true to the data. Re-validate your data if necessary. Never-ever ***ASSUME***. You know what they say... *it will always make an **ASS** out of **U** and **ME**. My momma is gonna get me for saying that.* Stay on track with the problem that you have decided to solve. Resist the temptation to draw *premature conclusions* due to pressure from management or even your own ego or biases. Ensure that you are providing timely updates to the proper forum of individuals who have expressed interest regarding the problem.

What other systems can be implicated?

This is an excellent time to begin to review your electrical schematics, system block diagrams and process flow charts if they are available. Simplifying complicated schematics into block diagrams is a great way to share system knowledge with everyone on your team. Electrical schematics can be very confusing for non-technical savvy team members. Attempt to translate your observations into simple terms for all to learn.

True Story: Keeping it simple

During a critical tool qualification, a piece of equipment mysteriously powered down. The technician hastily determined (Knee-Jerk Analysis) that the main power breaker was faulty, requiring assistance from another department to complete the repair. After retrieving the schematics and carefully studying the characteristics of the problem, within one hour we were able to locate a loose screw on an interlock panel that was causing an intermittent connection induced by vibrations from people who were working in the area.

***** CAUTION *****

- A ***Knee-Jerk Analysis*** is a hasty analysis that is made without carefully considering all the facts surrounding the problem.

- ***Analysis Paralysis*** sets in when all the data has been gathered. All reasonable questions have been answered but the team cannot agree on a solution to solve the problem.

What issues have been uncovered?

Begin to discuss your findings with others on your team for a second opinion. This will also indirectly involve your team during the troubleshooting process. This technique will build confidence within your team and increase the sharing of knowledge.

- Brainstorm all possible root-causes and issues that were uncovered.

- Attempt to have an explanation for all observations that were annotated during the *Problem Observation* phase.

- Begin to validate assumptions based upon theoretical knowledge. Challenge ideas to accelerate the process. ***Challenge the idea, not the individual.*** This process can get a little heated as egos began to surface for various reasons. The problem leader should attempt to keep everyone focused on the problem at hand. Do not allow the team to meander down a *rabbit trail*.

- Begin to separate plausible root-causes that could contribute to ***The*** problem from the ***A*** problems that will later be addressed. Remember, occasionally that your ***A*** problem will become ***The*** problem.

- Prioritize plausible root-causes according to their highest probability of failure based upon your observations and data.

Probability of Failures Priority

1. **Mechanical** - Parts such as bearings for motors will go bad due to normal wear and tear. Lubricants will degrade over time. Effective maintenance is vital to the longevity of these parts. Poor maintenance due to unqualified personnel or ambiguous procedures can cause the parts to fail prematurely.

2. **Electrical** - Wires don't usually degrade. However, they can be damaged due to improper routing during maintenance activities. They can become brittle because of overheating or become loose due to poor connections.

3. **Electronics** - Designed to last forever due to no moving parts. However, they can be damaged if they are not cared for properly. These delicate components are usually damaged due to overheating and ESD (Electro-Static Discharge) due to improper handling.

FYI: *Motors are electrical/mechanical devices that can fail in either mode.*

******CAUTION******

Beware of multiple problems that contribute to the same failure manifestation. I have solved some very elusive problems that sometimes had three or more minor problems that all resulted in a similar failure. Further analysis revealed that though similar, each failure was uniquely different, thus requiring a separate repair plan and testing scheme. An impatient problem-solver will usually overlook these small similarities.

Summary: Phase 3 Problem Analysis

- Establish an environment that will promote innovative ideas.
- Address all problems among team members.
- Brainstorm all issues that were uncovered.
- Characterize the nature of the failure – mechanical, electrical, electronic, temperature, or software.
- Remember the KISS principle.
- Attempt to explain all observations.
- Begin to formulate theories of possible failure items.
- Identity and prioritize factors that have the greatest probability of failure.
- Begin to *identify* the **A** problems to be addressed later.
- Identify and prioritize all areas of potential failure according to their impact to the root-cause.
- Make sure you are addressing the plausible root-causes and not the symptom or manifestation.
- Verify the accuracy of your data.
- Stay on track; resist the temptation to develop premature conclusions *(Knee-Jerk Analysis).*

Okay, let's apply our newfound knowledge to our gas heating problem.

Let's review...

Problem Statement: The heating system is not maintaining the desired temperature.

Problem Background: Winter has not yet begun. Funds are limited. Husband is willing and has time to work on the problem.

Problem Observation/*Analysis*:

1. The gas heating system is making a loud disturbing noise; like a sick moose.
   - *Possible mechanical binding.*

2. The blower will intermittently run ~2 hours before rapidly winding down to a halt. The blower began to make a loud hum before eventually shutting off.
   - *Possible electrical/mechanical part failure.*

3. The blower shaft can be turned by hand - no excessive binding was observed.
   - *No obvious or gross mechanical binding.*

4. Blower was covered in dust.
   - *Dust could cause overheating condition that could have increased degradation of the blower/motor.*

5. Air Filter was dirty.
   - *Filter needs to be replaced. A dirty air filter prevents a clean supply of air thus contributing to an overheating condition.*

6. All electrical connections were verified per the electrical schematic attached to panel; no discoloration, frayed or exposed wires were observed.
    - *No indication of overheating or damaged wires.*

7. All metering checks were good throughout the interlock sensors.
    - *No faulty interlock sensors.*

8. The gas ignition system was producing a sustainable flame.
    - *Gas system is working correctly.*

9. Once the blower stopped and began to hum, the flame/gas would remain on for about 10 minutes before the system would shut-down.
    - *The flame heat was not being forced through the duct system, thus eventually causing the duct temperature to overheat which caused the system to shut down. System is working correctly.*

10. After allowing the system to cool, it would sometimes start back up before eventually rotating rapidly to a halt. Sometimes the blower would simply begin making a loud humming sound.
    - *Part degradation characteristics - possible faulty blower circuit.*
    - *Frequency of failure – Conditional.*
    - *Failure category – Electrical.*

11. I noticed after the system shutdown, I was getting a series of blinking lights on the Controller (four blinking lights).
    - *According to the alarm matrix, the alarm over-temp failure is a result of the blower not forcing the flame heat throughout the duct system. If the over-temp sensor was faulty, it could produce an unpleasant condition in the duct system.*

12. An attached alarm matrix on the panel door indicated that the over-temp switch is faulty or an actual over-temp condition has been detected.
- *This was an actual over-temp condition because the alarm would eventually reset when the system cooled down.*

13. The last failure was due to a faulty over-temp switch (covered under warranty) two years ago.
- *Irrelevant to the problem. Over-temp sensor is performing correctly.*

14. The furnace has been in service for five years.
- *Parts will begin to wear and degrade in performance.*

15. I found a loose electrical wire that was not connected.
- *Per schematic drawing, the disconnected wire was added for an upgrade that was not installed.*

16. Current system configuration was programmed to allow the blower to operate continuously.
- *Possibly contributed to a premature failure by extending the operating time.*

17. System documentation was poor; only a basic component wiring diagram and alarm matrix was available on the panel.
- *Need to develop better documentation.*

Analysis Summary

- Interlocks are working correctly.

- Over-temp alarm is an actual failed condition due to the blower not working correctly.

- Nature of failure is **electrical** - Blower has begun to fail resulting from a possible degrading electrical magnetic field.

- Electrical wires and connections have not been compromised.

- Blower was in constant operation when heating unit was not needed, thus possibly contributing to a shorter system life span.

- Frequency of failure is **conditional** - It would run for about one hour after the system was allowed to remain idle for a few hours, essentially allowing the system to cool or temp down.

Plausible root-causes:

- Blower's magnetic field is failing.

- Blower's starter circuit (capacitor) is failing.

- Blower unit could be overheating due to dust accumulating on the unit over the last five years.

- Blower components have prematurely failed due to current system configuration.

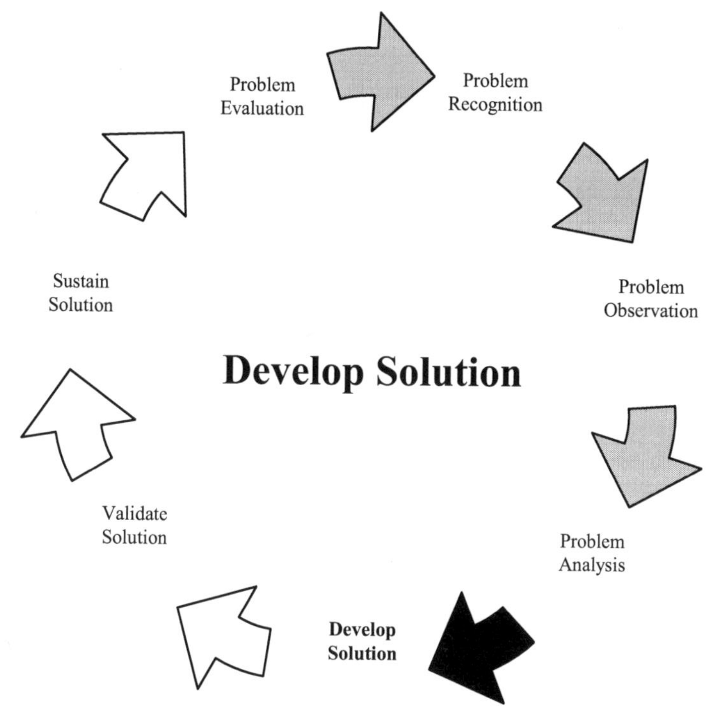
Problem
Evaluation
Problem
Recognition
Problem
Observation
Problem
Analysis
Develop
Solution
Validate
Solution
Sustain
Solution
Develop Solution

Chapter 5

Develop Solution

Plan your work then work your plan.

Many problem-solving efforts fail before they get started due to a lack of facts or hasty fact finding initiatives and improper analysis. Effective troubleshooting is **90%** fact-finding and **10%** actual work. Developing a successful plan is critical to the quick and safe recovery of the failed system or process. Occasionally, your most probable failure items will not be the first thing you perform based upon your associated risk and business needs. During the *Develop Solution* phase, we will focus upon strategies to develop the most effective solutions to resolve your issues and to satisfy your business objectives.

The True Cost of Downtime

How much is your solution going to cost your organization? Repair cost is a big concern for many organizations. Repair cost is usually the largest expenditure for most maintenance organizations. What is the true cost of downtime? How much revenue will be lost if this equipment or problem is allowed to be unresolved? Many technical professionals are oblivious of the true cost of equipment or process downtime. For example, after ordering a part... ask yourself; is the part really ordered? Do you have the part tracking information? Oftentimes everyone ***assumes*** that a part has been ordered only to discover that no one actually ordered the part. This miss extends the cost of downtime. *Action plans* must be followed through precisely to ensure the success of your strategies.

How will you test your theories? Strategies must be developed to test your proposed theories. I have evaluated tests that were not properly designed resulting into more confusion. As a result, the team traveled down a few more *rabbit trails* before they realized how much time they had wasted. For example, let's say you are working on an intermittent failure that usually fails within 45 minutes; it would be foolish to develop a 5 minute reliability test and prematurely declare victory.

Problem team leaders are ultimately responsible for overseeing the development of the plan and comprehending all the impacts to your objectives. Disclosing the details of your plan will enable your organization to maximize its efforts. For example, if the plan will potentially cause a bottle-neck or back-up within your production line, the factory managers can re-route product to reduce the impact.

For critical repairs that have high visibility, it behooves you to have a precise communication strategy that will enable you to promptly communicate your progress. It could be as simple as sending a text message to your direct manager or members of your team. From my experience, a quick text message reigns supreme. Managers and supervisors appreciate when they are informed of the late breaking news to effectively communicate to their managers. Accurate and timely communication will enable you to develop a sense of trust with all the key stakeholders of your team. Accurately forecasting the true cost of downtime and associated risks of your problem will demonstrate to your organization that you are capable of managing the problem.

What proposed solutions have you identified?

From your list of all possible causes, begin to prioritize the most probable components that have the strongest correlation to your problem. Stay on track. Write down the proposed solution and supporting theory. Oftentimes your initial theory may be weak, but don't let that stop you.

The only stupid question is the one that is not asked.

During the process of developing solutions, avoid ***the temptation to deviate from the data*** which you have methodically collected. It is at this time when technical professionals (especially the more senior ones) begin to reflect on past experiences that usually lead to the production of a nice *wish-list* rather than a concrete plan based upon accurate data.

Be very careful that you don't develop a solution that will negatively impact your progress, thus setting your team further back for days and sometimes weeks. Attempt to do the less intrusive and the most cost effective solutions first. Some solutions will require only a few minutes to perform while others will require a few hours or even days or weeks to evaluate (depending upon the magnitude of the problem and available resources). The priority of the solutions to perform doesn't have to align with the highest probability of failure, but rather is based upon the priorities, business impacts and objectives surrounding the problem. For example, if the most probable solution will cost $10,000 and three days to perform and evaluate, you may want to perform a probable solution that can be performed and evaluated within a few hours at minimum cost.

Simply put... perform the solutions that are the easiest to accomplish and have the greatest alignment to your business objectives. These solutions could be a simple part replacement to quickly validate a part performance. Major solutions such as equipment rebuilds are: costly, time consuming, and tend to induce other problems. *Remember, most equipment problems are self-induced.*

Ask questions regarding your proposed solutions among your peers. This is not the time to become a ***Lone-Ranger***. There is generally lots of untapped potential and knowledge among your team at your disposal. Remember, you are seeking for high agreement regarding the most effective solutions to invest your precious resources.

True Story: The Silent Storm

I vividly recall during one account almost missing the opportunity to practice what I preach. I was assigned to a team that was vigorously attempting to develop a long-term solution for a chronic problem that we were addressing. I noticed during the meeting that one ***individual was seemingly too quite****. I was told by others who managed him of how bright he really was; however, no one appeared too listen to his ideas. Being very familiar with recognizing and becoming a silent storm, I immediately attempted to engage this individual into the discussion. I solicited his opinions as an expert on the system and living with the problem everyday. After gaining his trust he murmured a suggestion. As anticipated, his idea was immediately challenged by the* ***Spin-Masters****. I smartly and publicly challenged the Spin-Masters to offer a better suggestion. They didn't have one. After winning the battle for my new friend, I asked him to give us the details of his proposal. To his surprise, I was in total agreement with his strategy because he was looking beyond our current capabilities by recommending a practical equipment modification to our system. His theory could be implemented and tested in a matter of hours. After assisting the development of a plan I empowered him to proceed with the implementation. His plan was successful. As a result, his plan was implemented as a solution for other groups as a permanent cost-effective solution to an old problem.*

I privately approached the individual regarding his seemingly well-thought-out and executed plan. He later told me that he had offered his idea as a solution months prior. However, no one took him seriously because it would have required an equipment modification and additional documentation to qualify as a permanent solution. This individual later became a key contributor to many technical problems in his group.

What are your team's boundary conditions?

Team boundary conditions are agreed upon conditions within your team to enable your team to expeditiously perform strategies with minimum impact to your problem-solving effort. Develop team boundary conditions that will promote harmony within the team and meet your business objectives. Boundary conditions are extremely important when the stakes are high to control the troubleshooting efforts. Too often, *lone-ranger* team members prefer to deviate from a well-thought-out strategy only to set the team efforts back. For example, to promote creativity I will usually set a boundary condition that would require the problem-owner's approval prior to deviating from a plan. Also, projects or experiments could be in progress to collect data without your knowledge. Your hasty decisions could invalidate the data collection scheme. Allow your engineers or team leaders to make the decision after carefully considering the impacts of your request.

True Story: Boundary Condition Violation

Previously, I referenced a problem team meltdown situation in which everyone had become frustrated due to the mounting pressure of the business conditions. ***Well, the incident got worse.*** *Upon the repair of the original problem, we imposed a few boundary conditions because the problem had multiple failure modes. Due to the design of the plan we were able to prevent any further changes to our system. The decision was made to enable the problem-team to conduct extra tests in an effort to properly characterize our problem. The boundary condition was requested as a temporary containment strategy.*

The boundary condition was simple; we requested that an external scheduled maintenance procedure which was an input into our system be postponed until we had fully evaluated our most recent failure.

Our intent was to baseline the system before proceeding with this scheduled maintenance activity. As a result, we were successfully able to characterize the recent failure to determine a containment strategy ***until...*** *a member of the team who had recently returned from vacation* ***authorized the forbidden maintenance activity*** *that was not to be performed until we had successfully base-lined the system. To no surprise to the original problem-team, the failure resurfaced causing the production lines to be once again shut down, thus potentially losing more revenue due to our inability to successfully ship product. To make matters worse the individual did not immediately disclose this information until we began to ask the question... What changed in our containment plan? As a result, an unnecessary task was performed, placing even more variability in our problem. The good news is that we were able to recover fairly quickly.*

Who can potentially be impacted by your solutions?

When formulating a strategy for a proposed solution, remember to consider all your resources. Many plans are not executed in a timely manner due to poor utilization of resources. Frequently, special tools for testing are omitted from the plan. Undocumented procedures or testing may require additional paperwork or approval. Oftentimes, action plans neglect to estimate the time requirements needed to incorporate other departments. In addition, other departments may have Service Level Agreements (SLAs) such as a 48-hour notification to secure a system before desired tasks are performed. For example, safety systems may have to be put in an idle state to perform work. Neglecting to get appropriate permission can cause a safety violation or put others at risk. Occasionally, special procedures are usually underestimated further delaying your efforts. As a result, a quick two-hour fix can rapidly become a 48-hour impact that may require additional resources. You may have to renegotiate your boundary conditions with your management team due to the additional time and resources required to execute and evaluate your proposed solution. Ensure that all affected stakeholders and customers are notified of your plans; get additional approval when appropriate.

What are the critical elements of your proposed solutions?

It's critical to determine all the specifics (who, what, when, where, how and cost) of your plan. Assign resources to your plan. Be specific as to what needs to happen. Develop a timeline or micro-schedule of when tasks should be completed so that you will be able to track the progress of your plan. Ensure that you have all the required test equipment, procedures, and spare parts available before executing your plan. Determine the total cost and impacts of your plan. You should factor such things as overtime, special services, and freight charges to expedite parts.

Poor planning on your part
does not constitute a crisis for others.

Is the proposed solution SAFE?

Determine if your plan can be safely executed without jeopardizing the equipment, product or personnel. Occasionally, you may have to develop additional procedures to ensure the safe execution of your plan. Ensure that your proposed solution does not violate your safety protocols. For example, during an occasion in which a 100-amp power distribution breaker was tripping off-line, a member of the team wanted to attempt to recreate the problem. I overruled this strategy due to the possibility of fostering an electrical fire potentially causing more equipment damage or personal injury.

Does your solution align with your business objectives?

Ensure that your plan aligns with your organization's business objectives. This is extremely important when resources are limited. Your plan should reduce any further damaging impacts to your organization. If your organization is cost-sensitive, you should attempt to define and prioritize the most cost-effective solution. For example, I recall one equipment failure that was the result of a broken user interface screen. This prevented the operator from executing commands on a touch screen rendering the equipment inoperative. Normally, this unit would have been simply replaced. The cost to replace the unit was $55,000. However, after considering the cost sensitive attitude of our organization and conducting a little more research with the original manufacturer, I was able to acquire the display unit for only $5,000. This was a cost-effective solution that aligned with the organization's cost objectives. Though it did take a little longer to get the system up to production, my cost avoidance was $50,000.

Who needs to be informed of your proposed solutions?

Many times we forget to develop a communication scheme to keep those who are interested up to date with the status of our efforts. I've found that most managers desire to have *too-much-information* rather than *too-little-information.* Prompt updates can allow you to spend more time executing your plan. Daily meetings are desired for problems that have a huge impact on your organization. As a general rule, I try to keep my immediate manager and those who express interest up to date regularly throughout the progression of my problem plan. If possible publish your plans and progress in a location where the information is available to all those who have a vested interest in the team’s success.

What is your action plan?

Each proposed solution should have a corresponding action plan. Your action plan should contain all the specific tasks or activities that are required to accurately evaluate the affect that the solution has on the problem. A well designed action plan will enable you to systematically remove variables from your problem and to identify if all assumed resources are available to support the solution. During the planning stage you may have to re-prioritize your solutions. The order of the task of your plan should be performed in such a way that avoids ambiguous results. Do the least intrusive task first. Once again, ensure that each task in your action plan can be safely performed to minimize risk to personnel, equipment, products, and business.

Your action plans should contain testing schemes that corresponds to the frequency of failure and nature of your problem. This is extremely important when you are dealing with intermittent or conditional failures. For example, if you have a system that fails after two hours of operation it would be unwise to deem a system repaired in the first 30 minutes of operation. The system should be allowed to operate without errors for at least six-to-eight hours. There are times when you may need to monitor the system performance for days or even weeks. Basically, you need to design a testing scheme that will align with your symptoms. Do not ***mask*** the real problem by developing ineffective testing schemes. I have witnessed this violation many times throughout my career. *Remember, you only get one time to make a first impression.*

During your planning, make sure that you have all the proper hand tools, test equipment, funds, and other resources to safely perform your task. Use the correct tool for the correct task to avoid inducing other problems. Don't use an oversized screwdriver for a small screw; you will most likely strip the head of the screw causing you more pain and time to properly remove it. For example, remember that simple home project that you wanted to do that was only going to take about 2 hours. Afterwards, due to poor planning you had to make numerous trips to your local home improvement store to complete the project. It most likely cost you more and took you longer than anticipated.

Effective plans will enable your team to be able to stay the course throughout the problem-solving effort. Well documented plans will enable you to revisit your team's previous conclusions to possibly determine new opportunities and gaps in your evaluations. Effective plans also will enable your team too accurately: communicate your progress, avoid time consuming detours, allow others to quickly join the problem-solving effort, and even assume the role of the problem-owner if necessary. In some situations, team members may be reassigned to support other pertinent business problems.

Summary: Phase 4 Develop Solution

- Comprehend the true cost of downtime.
- Develop solutions around your ***data supported*** theories.
- Solicit inputs from others regarding your solutions and plans.
- Develop or comprehend boundary conditions.
- Design solutions and plans that does not further impact the equipment, systems, or operations.
- Understand who will be impacted by your plan.
- Do the easy, less intrusive tasks first.
- Understand all required resources to support the plan.
- Ensure proposed solutions and plans are safe.
- Develop an effective test scheme.
- Develop strategies that align with your business objectives.
- Develop an effective communication strategy.

People don't plan to fail; they simply fail to plan.
- Unknown

Ok let's apply our newfound knowledge to our gas heating problem.

Let's review...

Problem: The heating system is not maintaining the desired temperature.

Background: Winter has not yet begun. Funds are limited. Husband is willing and has time to work on the problem.

Problem Observation/*Analysis*:

1. The gas heating system is making a loud disturbing noise; like a sick moose.
    - *Possible mechanical binding.*

2. The blower will intermittently run ~2 hours before rapidly winding down to a halt. The blower began to make a loud hum before eventually shutting off.
    - *Possible electrical/mechanical part failure.*

3. The blower shaft can be turned by hand - no excessive binding was observed.
    - *No obvious or gross mechanical binding.*

4. Blower was covered in dust.
    - *Dust could cause overheating condition that could have increased degradation of the blower/motor.*

5. Air Filter was dirty.
    - *Filter needs to be replaced. A dirty air filter prevents a clean supply of air thus contributing to an overheating condition.*

6. All electrical connections were verified per the electrical schematic attached to panel; no discoloration, frayed or exposed wires were observed.
- *No indication of overheating or damaged wires.*

7. All metering checks were good throughout the interlock sensors.
- *No faulty interlock sensors.*

8. The gas ignition system was producing a sustainable flame.
- *Gas system is working correctly.*

9. Once the blower stopped and began to hum, the flame/gas would remain on for about 10 minutes before the system would shut-down.
- *The flame heat was not being forced through the duct system, thus eventually causing the duct temperature to overheat which caused the system to shut down. System is working correctly.*

10. After allowing the system to cool, it would sometimes start back up before eventually rotating rapidly to a halt. Sometimes the blower would simply begin making a loud humming sound.
- *Part degradation characteristics - possible faulty blower circuit.*
- *Frequency of failure – Conditional.*
- *Failure category – Electrical.*

11. I noticed after the system shutdown, I was getting a series of blinking lights on the Controller (four blinking lights).
- *According to the alarm matrix, the alarm over-temp failure is a result of the blower not forcing the flame heat throughout the duct system. If the over-temp sensor was faulty, it could produce an unpleasant condition in the duct system.*

12. An attached alarm matrix on the panel door indicated that the over-temp switch is faulty or an actual over-temp condition has been detected.

- *This was an actual over-temp condition because the alarm would eventually reset when the system cooled down.*

13. The last failure was due to a faulty over-temp switch (covered under warranty) two years ago.

- *Irrelevant to the problem. Over-temp sensor is performing correctly.*

14. The furnace has been in service for five years.

- *Parts will begin to wear and degrade in performance.*

15. I found a loose electrical wire that was not connected.

- *Per schematic drawing, the disconnected wire was added for an upgrade that was not installed.*

16. Current system configuration was programmed to allow the blower to operate continuously.

- *Possibly contributed to a premature failure by extending the operating time.*

17. System documentation was poor; only a basic component wiring diagram and alarm matrix was available on the panel.

- *Need to develop better documentation.*

Analysis Summary

- Interlocks are working correctly.
- Over-temp is an actual fail condition due to the blower not working correctly.
- Nature of failure is **electrical** - Blower has begun to fail resulting from a possible degrading electrical magnetic field.
- Electrical wires and connections have not been compromised.
- Blower was in constant operation when heat unit was not needed, thus possibly contributing to a shorter system life span.
- Frequency of failure is **conditional** - It would run for about one hour after the system was allowed to remain idle for a few hours, essentially allowing the system to cool or temp down.

Plausible root-causes:

- Blower magnetic field is failing.
- Blower starter circuit (capacitor) is failing.
- Blower unit could be overheating due to dust accumulating on the unit over the last five years.
- Blower components have prematurely failed due to current system configuration.

Phase 4: Solutions

Solution #1 Pay for a service call

- **Effort level:** NA (Not Available)
- **Risk level:** NA.
- **Task duration:** Three hours.
- **Part availability:** NA.
- **Tools required:** NA.
- **Test equipment:** NA.
- **Test method:** NA.
- **Safety concerns:** Certified technician
    - Capacitors usually carry an electrical charge; therefore the component must be discharged to ground to dissipate stored energy.
    - Ergonomic concerns due to lying on one's back and side to carefully remove difficult screws.
    - Ensure electrical power is secure.
    - Ensure gas is properly secured, preventing unwanted activation.
- **Business impact:** The gas heating system is not yet required. We are still experiencing fall weather, which has moderate temperatures in Colorado. Urgency level is medium. With unpredictable weather, you don't want to be caught without a working furnace if a sudden snow storm decides to blow in.
- **Cost:** $2,000.
- **Advantage:** Warranty work.
- **Disadvantage:** Cost of a service call will only place additional burden on limited financial resources.

Action Plan: Pay for a service call

1. Place a service call.

Solution #2 Clean/rebuild blower unit

- **Effort level:** *Severe* - Unit will have to be removed from the duct system. Basically, the majority of the system will be disassembled.
- **Risk level:** Task could potentially induce more problems such as broken sensors or wires due to the nature of the task.
- **Task duration:** Three hours.
- **Part availability:** NA.
- **Tools required:** Standard screwdriver, vacuum cleaner, and machine lubricant.
- **Test equipment:** Standard voltage tester to check for power.
- **Test method:** Clean and lubricate blower unit. Allow system to run for two days without errors.
- **Safety concerns:**
  - Capacitors usually carry an electrical charge; therefore the component must be discharged to an electrical ground to dissipate stored energy.
  - Ergonomic concerns due to lying on one's back and side to carefully remove difficult screws.
  - Ensure electrical power is secure.
  - Ensure gas is properly secured, preventing unwanted activation.
- **Business impact:** The gas heating system is not yet required. We are still in fall weather, which has moderate temperatures in Colorado. Urgency level is medium. With unpredictable weather, you don't want to be caught without a working furnace, in the event that a snow storm should suddenly decide to blow in.
- **Cost:** NA.
- **Advantage:** Most cost effective.
- **Disadvantage:** The potential to induce other problems.

Action Plan: Clean/rebuild blower unit

1. Secure power and gas to the system. Ensure that no one will accidentally energize the system while you are performing work.
2. Discharge capacitor by shorting leads with a grounding probe or an insulated screwdriver. You may see a small spark from the capacitor.
3. Verify the system is safe to perform task. Perform meter checks and look for illuminated indicators.
4. Safely remove and label (if required) all electrical wires to ensure the proper connections.
5. Safely remove all mounting screws.
6. Safely remove the blower unit from the furnace enclosure.
7. Safely remove the cover screws from the blower.
8. Conduct a visual inspection. Look for signs of overheating such as charred wires or brittle cables. Also look for wire damage such as exposed electrical wires. Replace as necessary.
9. Inspect for excessive binding of the motor while manually turning the shaft.
10. Use vacuum to remove all excessive dust from unit.
11. Apply a lubricating substance to the shaft of motor to allow bearings to move freely.
12. Safely re-install blower unit.
13. Connect mounting screws.
14. Connect electrical wires.
15. Re-apply power and gas.
16. Run unit until next failure.

Solution #3 Replace blower starter circuit

- **Effort level:** Requires *minimum* effort. A few wires will need to be disconnected. The oil filled capacitor is only mounted by two screws.
- **Task duration:** One hour.
- **Risk level:** NA.
- **Part availability:** Part will have to be special ordered from the manufacturer in Florida. Overnight shipping required.
- **Tools required:** Standard screwdriver.
- **Test equipment:** Standard voltage tester.
- **Test method:** Replace component and energize system. Allow system to run for two days without errors.
- **Safety concerns:**
    - Capacitors usually carry an electrical charge; therefore the component must be discharged to an electrical ground to dissipate stored energy.
    - Secure electrical power (120 volts).
    - Secure gas supply.
    - Ergonomics - minimum bending required.
- **Business impact:** The gas heating system is not required yet. We are still experiencing fall weather, which has moderate temperatures in Colorado. Urgency level is medium. With unpredictable weather, you don't want to be caught without a working furnace if a sudden snow storm decides to blow in.
- **Cost:** $20.
- **Advantage:** Low cost.
- **Disadvantage:** Part has to be special ordered. Part will arrive in two days.

Action Plan: Replace blower starter circuit

1. Order part.
2. Inspect part for obvious defects.
3. Secure power and gas to the system. Ensure that no one will accidentally energize the system while you are performing work.
4. Discharge capacitor by shorting leads with a grounding probe or an insulated screwdriver. You may see a small spark from the capacitor.
5. Verify the system is safe to perform task. Perform meter checks and look for illuminated indicators.
6. Safely remove and label (if required) all electrical wires to ensure the proper connections.
7. Remove old part.
8. Install new part.
9. Reconnect electrical wires.
10. Run to next failure.

Solution #4 Replace blower unit

- **Effort level:** *Severe* - Unit will have to be removed from duct system. Basically, the majority of the system will be disassembled.
- **Risk level:** Action could potentially induce more issues such as broken sensors or wires due to nature of the task.
- **Task duration:** Three hours.
- **Part availability:** Compatible part is available at a local heating store.
- **Tools required:** Standard screwdriver.
- **Test equipment:** Standard voltage tester to check for power.
- **Test method:** Replace unit. Allow system to run for two days without errors.
- **Safety concerns:**
  - Capacitors usually carry an electrical charge; therefore the component must be discharged to an electrical ground to dissipate stored energy.
  - Ergonomic concerns due to lying on one's back and side to carefully remove difficult screws.
  - Ensure electrical power is secured.
  - Ensure gas is properly secured, preventing unwanted activation.
- **Business impact:** The gas heating system is not yet required. We are still in fall weather which has moderate temperatures in Colorado. Urgency level is medium. With unpredictable weather, you don't want to be caught without a working furnace if a sudden snow storm decides to blow in.
- **Cost:** $120.
- **Advantage:** Warranty part.
- **Disadvantage:** The potential to induce other problems and high-cost.

Action Plan: Replace blower unit

1. Purchase part.
2. Inspect part for obvious defects.
3. Secure power and gas to the system. Ensure that no one will accidentally energize the system while you are performing work.
4. Discharge capacitor by shorting leads with a grounding probe or an insulated screwdriver. You may see a small spark from the capacitor.
5. Verify the system is safe to perform task. Perform meter checks and look for illuminated indicators.
6. Safely remove and label (if required) all electrical wires to ensure the proper connections.
7. Safely remove all mounting screws.
8. Safely remove the blower unit from the furnace enclosure.
9. Safely remove the cover screws from the blower.
10. Safely remove old blower unit.
11. Safely re-install new blower unit.
12. Connect mounting screws.
13. Connect electrical wires.
14. Re-apply power and gas.
15. Run unit until next failure.

Prioritize Solutions

Prioritize solutions to meet your business objectives which are ***cost*** and ***medium urgency*** due to current weather conditions:

1. **Clean/rebuild blower** - No cost.
2. **Replace starter circuit** - $20.
3. **Replace blower** - $120.
4. **Place service call** - $2,000.

Assessment	Pay for Service Call	Clean/Rebuild Blower	Replace Blower Starter	Replace Blower Unit
Effort Level	NA	*Severe* - Unit will have to be removed from duct system. Basically, the majority of the system will be disassembled.	Requires *minimum* effort. A few wires will need to be disconnected. The oil filled capacitor is only mounted by two screws.	*Severe* - Unit will have to be removed from duct system. Basically, the majority of the system will be disassembled.
Risk Level	NA	Induce other problems.	Induce other problems.	Induce other problems.
Task Duration	Three hours.	Three hours.	One hour.	One hour.
Part Availability	NA	NA	Special overnight order	Local electrical store
Tools Required	NA	Standard screwdriver, vacuum cleaner and machine lubricant.	Standard screwdriver.	Standard screwdriver.
Test Equipment	NA	Standard voltage tester to check for power.	Standard voltage tester to check for power.	Standard voltage tester to check for power.
Test Method	NA	Clean and lubricate unit. Allow system to run for two days without errors.	Replace component and energize system. Allow system to run for two days without errors.	Replace component and energize system. Allow system to run for two days without errors.
Safety Concerns	Energized capacitors. Ergonomics. De-energize electrical power.	Energized capacitors. Ergonomics. De-energize electrical power.	Energized capacitors. Ergonomics. De-energize electrical power.	Energized capacitors. Ergonomics. De-energize electrical power.
Business Impacts	The heating system is not yet required. We are still experiencing fall weather which has moderate temperatures in Colorado.	The heating system is not yet required. We are still experiencing fall weather which has moderate temperatures in Colorado.	The heating system is not yet required. We are still experiencing fall weather which has moderate temperatures in Colorado.	The heating system is not yet required. We are still experiencing fall weather which has moderate temperatures in Colorado.
Cost	$2,000	NA	$20	$120
Advantages	Warranty work.	Most cost effective.	Inexpensive.	Warranty part.
Disadvantages	Additional burden on limited financial resources.	Potentially induce other problems.	Special order - two days.	Potentially induce other problems.

Solution Table-4-1

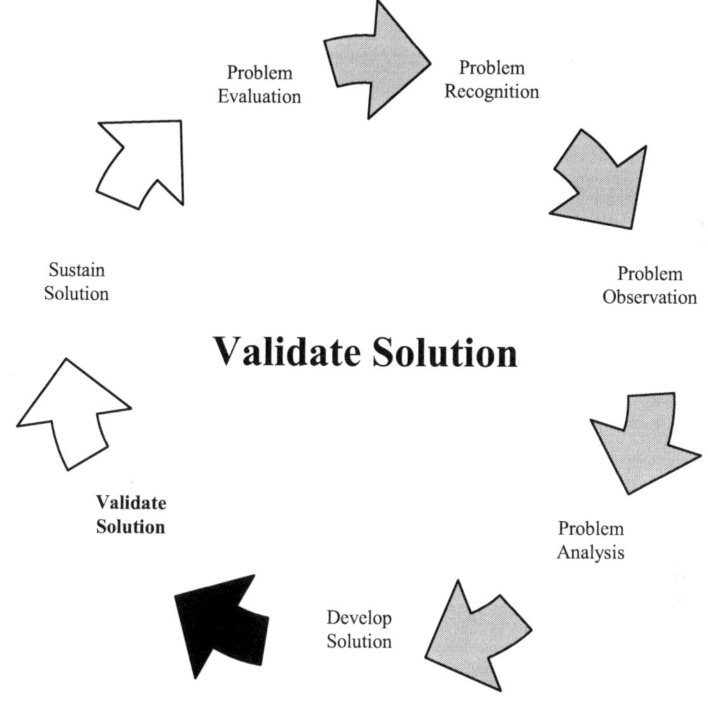
Problem
Evaluation
Problem
Recognition
Sustain
Solution
Problem
Observation
Validate Solution
Validate
Solution
Problem
Analysis
Develop
Solution

Chapter 6

Validate Solution

Change is not change until it is change.
- Edwin Lewis Cole

We are ready to execute our plan now that we have properly evaluated the problem, gathered all available information surrounding the problem, analyzed the data and developed strategic solutions that are in alignment with our business objectives. It is at this point when your team should be excited to begin to implement their solutions. Did you actually repair the problem? A problem that has been carefully characterized can be properly solved. It is during the *Validate Solution* phase of the process when you actually begin to do the ***real work***; the **10%** I referred to earlier. Now we are prepared to systematically implement our solutions to evaluate their impact to the problem.

I have been in team meetings in which members have attempted to say their hasty solutions made the problem a ***little-better***. A ***little-better*** was not the goal. Or, occasionally someone will make the comment that... *we don't know what really fixed the problem because we did a* ***bunch-of-things***. This answer is likewise unacceptable. I refer to these folks as the *Spin-Masters.* They attempt to spin every story from the truth by casting doubt. Oddly enough, they rarely bring any concrete data or ideas to the team for discussion. They almost immediately attack most ideas with no regards to the supporting data with comments like... ***we have tried that before... it won't work***. Remember, we are trying to identify the root-cause of the problem... not a ***quick fix, band-aid or mask***. Stick to your plan.

To what extent has the solution(s) eliminated the problem?

Stay true to your plan and the results of each solution. Either you have solved the problem or you didn't. ***It is what it is***. Execute your plan with precision so that you can carefully understand your impacts.

Have desired goals been achieved and boundary conditions met?

Make sure that you have a good reason for not remaining within your agreed upon boundary conditions. It is usually a *bitter-sweet* situation if you solve a problem by violating boundary conditions such as safety, quality controls or specification violations. I have witnessed well intended ideas that have backfired on individuals who place production output over safety. Your priorities should be ***Safety-Quality-Output***. You can never go wrong with this decision making philosophy.

Have results been properly documented?

As previously discussed, ensure that your progress has been carefully documented. Ensure that you will be able to accurately surmise your information to determine if there are other concerns uncovered that require further testing and discussions. You need to hold your team accountable for proper documentation. You should regularly inspect your team's ability to properly adhere to your documentation strategy. Every problem is a learning opportunity.

People don't do what's Expected,
People do what's Inspected.

- Bob Harrison
Motivational Speaker

Did any side affects occur?

Make sure that you are not simultaneously implementing solutions in order to expedite your results. In doing so, you limit your ability to fully determine which solution truly solved or affected your problem. It is common to group tasks if they have similar impacts and have the same associated risks. Executing a methodical designed plan will ensure that you are able to determine if any positive or negative side affects were introduced into your existing problem. Also, you will be able to counter-spin the *Spin-Masters* later. I have seen many troubleshooting efforts abandoned due to undocumented side effects that were introduced unawares into a problem.

Does a contingency plan need to be developed?

If your problem is not resolved, be prepared to re-visit some of your conclusions during your analysis. ***Don't throw the baby out with the bath water***. Do not feel as though you have wasted your time. Your team has invested lots of time (usually long hours away from their families) to the complete resolution of this problem. It will be imperative that you confidently lead them back into a brain-storming session to comprehend the results of the action plans. Every variable that you eliminate will put you one step closer to solving your problem.

Do you need to investigate the problem and its cause further?

Occasionally, problems are resolved without a clear understanding of exactly how your solution solved the problem. This has been my experience in the high technology industry. I vividly recall after solving a major excursion taking approximately two weeks to fully comprehend the impact of our solution. As stated previously, do not allow a weak theory to stop you from developing a strategy. If you have some confidence that you can eliminate some variables and add some insight to the problem; *go for it*. Strive to fully understand the results so that you can apply your newfound knowledge later.

Insanity is doing the same thing
the same way expecting different results.

Don't *Mask* the problem

Masking the problem is a real problem in our technical community; we hear about it all the time. Masking problems results from an improper characterization of the original problem. If a problem is not determined to be intermittent or conditional, it can be marginally repaired. For example, if the failure occurs after one hour of operation it will sound ludicrous to conclude that a problem has been repaired within 15 minutes of implementing a solution. I wish I could say this is a rare occurrence, but I can't. Masking problems also occurs when we knowingly violate other specifications or intentionally conduct unauthorized procedures to make the original problem appear to be solved. *Masking will always come back to bite you in the end.* For example, I recall during one occasion in which safety devices were altered by the technicians because the operators kept complaining of the constant alarms that were annoying them. Long-story short... the alarms were real. Fortunately, no one was hurt.

Ensure that your plan is being executed precisely so that you can properly validate your results to determine your progress. Frequently, during troubleshooting a bad part or measurement can send you down the wrong path. However, a well-documented plan can logically navigate you back on the correct path.

True Story: Bad Printed Circuit Boards

While in the Navy, I troubleshot a problem in which I encountered five faulty printed circuit boards (PCBs). I was very proud of myself when I troubleshot the problem the first time, only to insert a faulty part. So I troubleshot back to the same part. I repeated the insane approach three more times before I finally got a properly repaired circuit board. Basically, I'm trying to say ***The Data Don't Lie****. Trust yourself; don't throw away a great troubleshooting effort for a shortcut. As the late attorney Johnny Cochran said,* ***If it doesn't fit... you must acquit.*** *Challenge your assumptions to determine if there are gaps in your theories.*

Occasionally, you will have to reinvestigate your theories further to better understand the reasons why you have apparently solved the problem. In my opinion, nothing is worse than unexplained repairs. They will usually come back to haunt you later. Spend the time to fully comprehend the affects of your solutions. This becomes extremely important if you have to report or present your findings to your managers. Throughout my career, I can admit that managers are very impressed when engineers and technicians are able to reassure them that a problem or excursion was properly mitigated.

Summary: Phase 5 Validate Solution

- ***The Data Don't Lie.***
- Validate results.
- Do not violate boundary conditions.
- Document all of your results.
- Develop contingency plans.
- Don't *Mask* the problem.
- Revisit your data and plans.

Okay, let's apply our newfound knowledge to our heating system problem.

Let's review...

Problem: The heating system is not maintaining the desired temperature.

Background: Winter has not yet begun. Funds are limited. Husband is willing and has time to work on the problem.

Problem Observation/*Analysis*:

1. The gas heating system is making a loud disturbing noise; like a sick moose.
   - *Possible mechanical binding.*

2. The blower will intermittently run ~2 hours before rapidly winding down to a halt. The blower began to make a loud hum before eventually shutting off.
   - *Possible electrical/mechanical part failure.*

3. The blower shaft can be turned by hand - no excessive binding was observed.
   - *No obvious or gross mechanical binding.*

4. Blower was covered in dust.
   - *Dust could cause overheating condition that could have increased degradation of the blower/motor.*

5. Air Filter was dirty.
   - *Filter needs to be replaced. A dirty air filter prevents a clean supply of air thus contributing to an overheating condition.*

6. All electrical connections were verified per the electrical schematic attached to panel; no discoloration, frayed or exposed wires were observed.
   - *No indication of overheating or damaged wires.*

7. All metering checks were good throughout the interlock sensors.
   - *No faulty interlock sensors.*

8. The gas ignition system was producing a sustainable flame.
   - *Gas system is working correctly.*

9. Once the blower stopped and began to hum, the flame/gas would remain on for about 10 minutes before the system would shut-down.
   - *The flame heat was not being forced through the duct system, thus eventually causing the duct temperature to overheat which caused the system to shut down. System is working correctly.*

10. After allowing the system to cool, it would sometimes start back up before eventually rotating rapidly to a halt. Sometimes the blower would simply begin making a loud humming sound.
    - *Part degradation characteristics - possible faulty blower circuit.*
    - *Frequency of failure – Conditional.*
    - *Failure category – Electrical.*

11. I noticed after the system shutdown, I was getting a series of blinking lights on the Controller (four blinking lights).
    - *According to the alarm matrix, the alarm over-temp failure is a result of the blower not forcing the flame heat throughout the duct system. If the over-temp sensor was faulty, it could produce an unpleasant condition in the duct system.*

12. An attached alarm matrix on the panel door indicated that the over-temp switch is faulty or an actual over-temp condition has been detected.

- *This was an actual over-temp condition because the alarm would eventually reset when the system cooled down.*

13. The last failure was due to a faulty over-temp switch (covered under warranty) two years ago.

- *Irrelevant to the problem. Over-temp sensor is performing correctly.*

14. The furnace has been in service for five years.

- *Parts will begin to wear and degrade in performance.*

15. I found a loose electrical wire that was not connected.

- *Per schematic drawing, the disconnected wire was added for an upgrade that was not installed.*

16. Current system configuration was programmed to allow the blower to operate continuously.

- *Possibly contributed to a premature failure by extending the operating time.*

17. System documentation was poor; only a basic component wiring diagram and alarm matrix was available on the panel.

- *Need to develop better documentation.*

Analysis Summary

- Interlocks are working correctly.

- Over-temp is an actual fail condition due to the blower not working correctly.

- Nature of failure is **electrical** - Blower has begun to fail resulting from a possible degrading electrical magnetic field.

- Electrical wires and connections have not been compromised.

- Blower was in constant operation when heat unit was not needed, thus possibly contributing to a shorter system life span.

- Frequency of failure is **conditional** - It would run for about one hour after the system was allowed to remain idle for a few hours, essentially allowing the system to cool or temp down.

Plausible root-causes:

- Blower magnetic field is failing.

- Blower starter circuit (capacitor) is failing.

- Blower unit could be overheating due to dust accumulating on the unit over the last five years.

- Blower components have prematurely failed due to current system configuration.

4: Proposed Solution

Align plans to meet your business objective and conditions which are cost and medium urgency due to current weather conditions:

1. **Clean/rebuild blower** - No cost.
2. **Replace starter circuit** - $20.
3. **Replace blower** - $120.
4. **Place service call** - $2,000.

5: Validate Solutions:

1. Clean/rebuild blower - Unit was safely removed and cleaned. Unit had an excessive amount of dust. Shaft did not turn smoothly. Shaft and bearings were lightly lubricated with machine oil. Unit reassembled and safely re-installed.

- **Results:** Unit ran normally for about six hours before resulting in the same loud sound and an abrupt stop of the blower. Unfortunately, it was at 3:00 a.m. so I simply secured the power to put the system in a *safe-state*.

2. Replaced starter circuit - Part was ordered and over-nighted from the OEM (Original Equipment Manufacturer). Part was safely installed.

- **Results:** Unit ran normally for 24 hours before yielding the same result. ***Darn it!!***

3. Replaced blower - Went to local heating parts store to purchase part. Blower came with a starter circuit, which was the standard practice per the salesman. Part was bench tested to ensure that it was working properly. Old part was safely removed and new part was safely installed.

- **Results:** Unit started up with no issues. The sound of the blower was significantly quieter than the original unit. Unit ran successfully for two days without any issues. Unit ran successfully throughout one of the worst winters in Colorado.

- Problem was resolved within our limited budget and prior to the winter.

- Racked up plenty of *brownie-points* with my family, especially with my wife.

Solution	Cost	Action Taken	Results	Comments
Clean/Rebuild Blower	$0	Unit was safely removed and cleaned. Removed excessive dust from unit. Shaft did not turn smoothly. Shaft and bearings were lightly lubricated with machine oil. Unit reassembled and safely reinstalled.	Unit ran normally for about six hours before resulting in the same loud sound and an abrupt stop of the blower. Unfortunately, it was at 3:00 a.m. so I simply secured the power to put the system in a *safe-state*.	KISS
Replace Starter Circuit	$20	Part was ordered and over-nighted from the manufacturer. Part was safely installed.	Unit ran normally for 24 hours before yielding the same result.	Darn it!!
Replace Blower	$120	Went to local heating parts store to purchase part. Blower came with a starter circuit (standard practice) per the salesman. Part was bench tested to ensure that it was working properly. Old part was safely removed and new part was safely installed.	Unit started up with no issues. The sound of the blower was significantly quieter than the original unit. Unit ran successfully for two days without any issues. Unit ran successfully throughout one of the worse winters in Colorado.	Problem was resolved within our limited budget and prior to the winter. Racked up plenty of *brownie-points* with my family, especially with my wife.
Place Service Call	$2,000	NA	NA	NA

Validate Solution Table 5-1

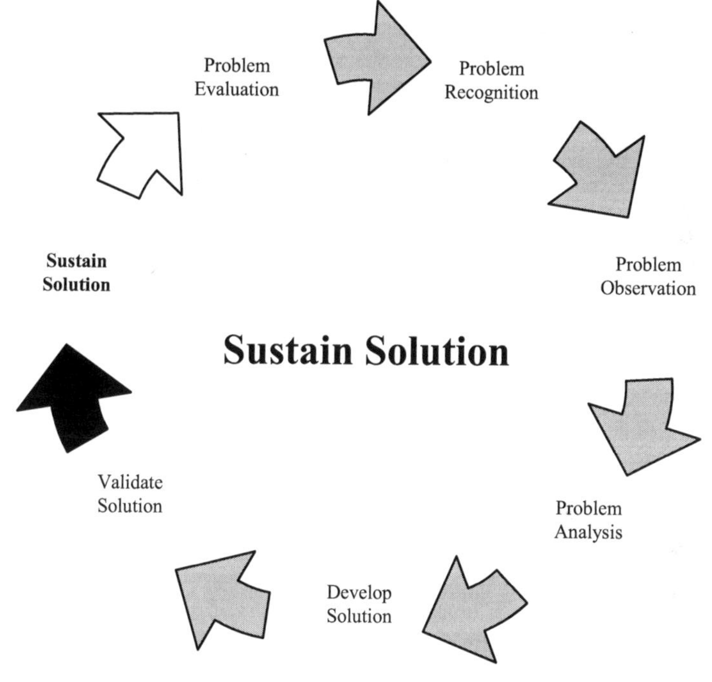
Problem
Evaluation
Problem
Recognition
Problem
Observation
Problem
Analysis
Develop
Solution
Validate
Solution
Sustain
Solution
Sustain Solution

Chapter 7

Sustain Solution

People who don't learn from their mistakes are destined to repeat them.

Congratulations!!! You effectively *solved* your problem while achieving your business objectives. *Or did you?* Most problem teams neglect this phase of the process. It is as important as the previous phases. Sustaining a solution is critical in a continuous improvement environment. This is a great opportunity to make changes in your maintenance scheduling or business process to ensure that your new knowledge is protected and documented. Knowledge is power in our competitive business environment. Successfully completing this phase of the process ensures the **lessons-learned** are accurately annotated for future reference in the equipment history. Response Flow Charts (RFCs) and procedures can be revised or created to reflect your new knowledge of the system. Remember every problem is a *learning opportunity*. During the *Sustain Solution* phase, you will learn the importance of standardizing your solutions to ensure problems are properly contained.

How will you integrate changes into your team?

Frequently, good ideas are simply lost due to ambiguous integration processes that are entangled with too much unnecessary bureaucracy. Ensure that your newfound knowledge is properly integrated into your team. Seek your team's input to discover sustaining proposals, especially those involved in the problem-solving effort. *Get high agreement*! These are team decisions; acceptance and consistent follow-up are much more likely to occur when people are involved in the early stages. This is a great opportunity to train other members on your team.

What documentation will you need?

Ensure that all the proper documentation is submitted to ensure that your new knowledge is properly recorded. This is the time to update or write new procedures or specifications to capture your new knowledge. This valuable information can be used to develop a troubleshooting response flow chart to assist in future troubleshooting efforts. Sharing your newfound knowledge with other groups through detailed presentations or training materials can demonstrate your ability to be a visionary for your organization. I have developed and presented many presentations throughout my career that have opened other doors of opportunities for me to advance my career further.

True Story: Now What?

I was approached after a problem-solving seminar by a gentleman regarding an IT related problem that he was trying to solve. He was on a tech-support team supporting many clients throughout the world. I gave him some advice regarding the specific technical problem that he presented. Months later he called me to inform me that he had followed my strategy to discover a solution to his problem. I asked the question... now what? He pondered then asked me what I was referring too. I asked him how he was going to protect, sustain, and share the new knowledge that he had learned. He said that there was no system in place to share the knowledge that his tech-support team was solving for their customers. I then told him that he just discovered an opportunity to develop a system and process for his team to share the knowledge. I advised him to research and develop a proposal for his management team to consider. He successfully developed a problem-solving database and a process for his team to enter and extract data. As a direct result of his efforts he was promoted.

Real leaders see problems as opportunities to improve.

Who is responsible for sustaining the improvements?

It has been my experience that you must assign a name and a date to the completion of tasks. This individual should be knowledgeable of the problem and usually an active member of the problem team. Make sure that you hold your team accountable to ensure that these tasks are completed in a timely manner. Resist the temptation not to effectively sustain your solution. Occasionally, you may have to de-prioritize your work or delegate this task to someone else. Make sure that you have an inspection system in place. Remember, *people don't do what's expected, but rather what's inspected.*

Who is responsible for providing training?

It is important to provide timely training to your team so that the knowledge does not become *tribal knowledge.* ***Tribal knowledge*** is pertinent information that only a few are privy to know. This is ineffective in a team environment. Unfortunately, it is a common practice among technical teams today. Some refer to it as job security. In my opinion, it is *job insecurity*. Don't get me wrong; in our competitive environment I do understand why people don't share all their knowledge. This strategy is not beneficial to the team. It has always been my strategy to work myself out of a job. To achieve my goal, I'm constantly sharing my knowledge with my teams.

Do you need to make *authorized* equipment modifications?

Occasionally, your containment strategy will involve equipment or process modifications. Ensure that your solutions are within your organization's safety and OEM (original equipment manufacturers) specifications. Unauthorized equipment modifications could cause potential safety issues and void warranties. Equipment modifications usually lead to other issues. Make sure you carefully evaluate all the possible impacts of your sustaining plan.

Summary: Phase 6 Sustain Solution

- Ensure procedures and response flow checklists are updated and technicians are receiving appropriate notifications.

- Develop strategies to share new knowledge with your team.

- Assign names and completion dates to tasks.

- Include engineers and team members in the improvement process.

- Work within your team for further equipment modifications and recommendations.

- Document all your work.

Now back to our furnace problem...

Our troubleshooting efforts have been successful thus far. Now that we have properly:

- Defined the problem.
- Obtained a thorough understanding of the system.
- Conducted a thorough observation of the conditions surrounding the problem.
- Conducted a detailed analysis of the data.
- Developed solutions and executed our plans according to our aligned objectives.

It is time to sustain this solution to ensure that we do not have to repeat our efforts again.

Let's recap... during our initial exposure to this problem we had minimal documentation. We only had a general wiring diagram and an alarm matrix that was affixed to the control panel. To improve this situation, I decided to create four new documents to assist in future problem-solving endeavors.

Process Flow Description

1. When the *Thermostat* (mercury) set point is out of range a 24 volt signal is sent to the *Controller* that begins the heating process.

2. The *Controller* ensures that all the safety features are not compromised (such as doors and over-temp switches). An open door will actually remove 115 volts from the circuit thus preventing the sequence to be completed. If the sensor or interlocks are compromised anytime during the process, the system will shut down.

3. If no sensor compromise is detected, the *Exhaust Fan* will be energized with 115 volts.

4. The *Controller* checks the pressure switch that is attached to the *Exhaust Fan* to ensure that the exhaust fan is operating.

5. If no sensor or interlocks are compromised, the *Controller* will then send 24 volts to energize the *Gas Igniter* (burner).

6. The *Controller* sends 24 volts to the *Gas Valve* to allow gas to flow into the *Gas Igniter* to convert the gas into a flame.

7. The *Controller* senses a signal from the *flame sensor* that a flame is present.

8. The *Controller* sends 115 volts to the *Blower Motor* to force hot air throughout the ventilation ducts.

9. The *Controller* checks the *over-temp limit switch* to ensure the *Blower* has turned on and is actually forcing the flamed heated air throughout the duct system. If an over-temp condition is sensed due to a faulty blower circuit, the system will shut down.

10. Once the desired temperature has been achieved, the thermostat will remove the 24 volts from the *Controller* to stop the process. The *Blower* will usually remain on for a set amount of time to ensure that all the heated air is evacuated from the air duct system.

Gas Heating System Theory of Operation

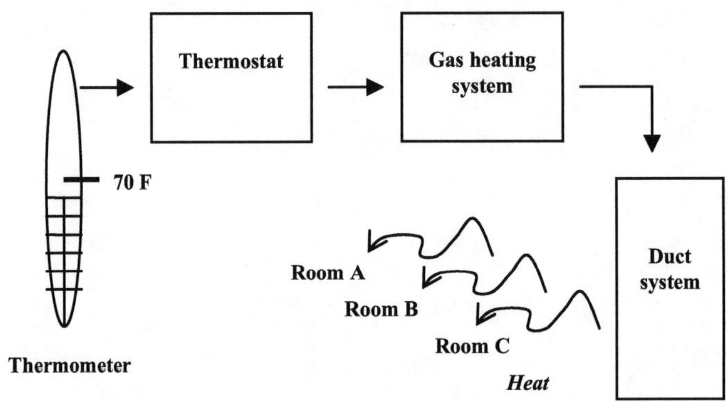

Diagram 6-1

Simplified Heater Process Flow Chart

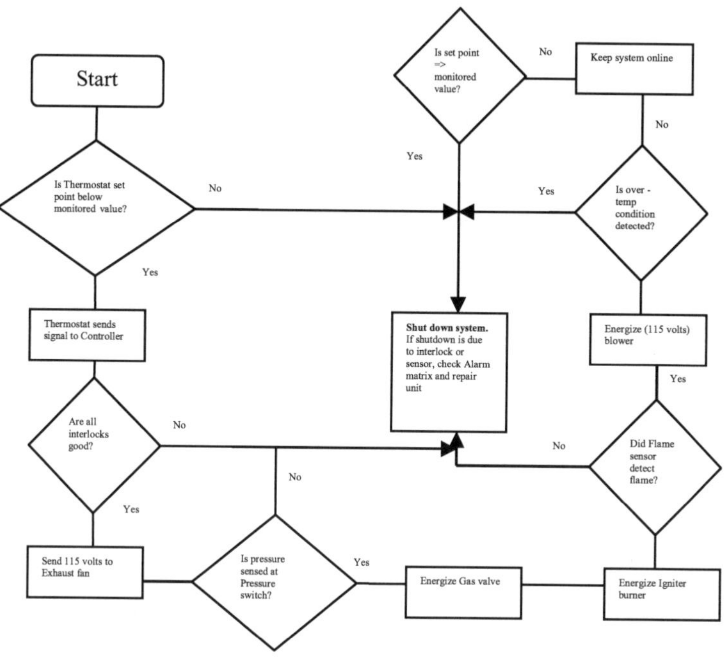

Diagram 6-2

Simplified Heating System Diagram

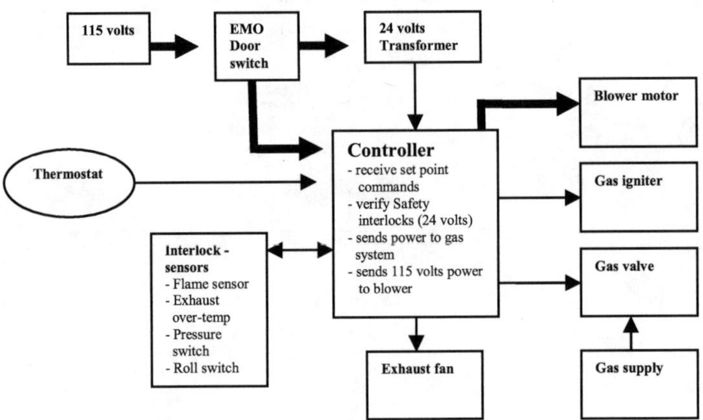

Diagram 6-3

Status Light (LED)	Equipment Problem	Check
On	Normal operation	-
One Blink	Ignition failure	• Gas flow • Gas pressure • Gas valve • Flame sensor
Two Blinks	Closed pressure switch	• Pressure switch failure • Bad connection
Three Blinks	Pressure switch failed to close	• Exhaust fan not energized • Pressure switch • Vent blockage
Four Blinks	Open over-temp limit switch	• Over-temp switch is opened • Over-temp is detected • Vent blockage
Five Blinks	False flame sensed	• Sticking gas valve • Faulty sensor
Rapid Continuous Blinking	Incorrect primary polarity	• Reversed transformer secondary • Reversed primary wires

Alarm Code Matrix Table 6-1

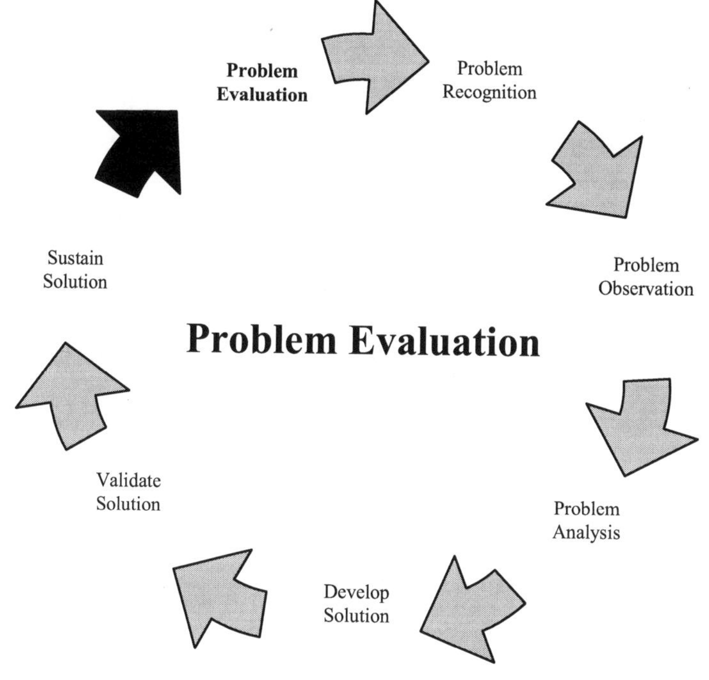
Problem Evaluation
Problem Recognition
Problem Observation
Problem Analysis
Develop Solution
Validate Solution
Sustain Solution
Problem Evaluation

Chapter 8

Problem Evaluation

Intention without Action is Insufficient.
- Dr. Geneva Gay
Educator

Awesome!! You have done an excellent job. You have now solved your problem and have successfully placed some countermeasures in place to better comprehend a similar problem if it reoccurs in the future. The *Problem Evaluation* phase of the process should be addressed as a team. It will help the team's progression to become a better team. A thorough problem evaluation will uncover other valuable opportunities to resolve. Spend some time evaluating the *Why's* of your problem. Ask yourself... *What did we really learn?* Also, you may expose other concerns regarding your team's overall performance.

A well-planned problem-solving effort usually uncovers many other questions or concerns that may need to be addressed. I previously referred to these as the ***A*** problems. An ***A*** problem is a problem that does not currently impact the operation of the equipment or process. However, if not properly addressed it can become ***The*** problem later. For example, a part can be making an abnormal sound, which is usually an indication of degradation or some form of misalignment.

True Story: Bad Repair Loop

A proper evaluation of a failure could indicate that you have other hidden issues. For example, I troubleshot an equipment problem only to discover that we were not effectively controlling the temperature of the system for our application. It was also discovered that we were not properly repairing the problems in the repair loop. After speaking with my manager, I was able to visit the repair/calibration lab to audit how they repaired the units. To my astonishment, I also discovered that they were not properly recreating the original problem, thus not actually repairing the systems. As a result of my audit, we established a new partnership with the repair lab in which the actual failure of the units was properly annotated so that the repair lab could accurately repair the system. The extra time invested actually uncovered a greater problem that was costing my organization a lot of money and wasted man-hours. We were replacing these expensive parts like cheap AA batteries. This problem was costing my organization tens of thousands of dollars a year.

Did you meet your objectives?

How often do we really evaluate this question? If your objectives are established during the *Problem Recognition* phase you will be able to answer this question. Measuring your team's performance to your business objectives can expose issues regarding the availability of resources such as funds, personnel or span of control. As stated previously, it is a *bitter-sweet* victory if you solve the problem but did not meet your business objectives. This is usually referred to as ***opportunity loss***. Opportunity loss in economic terms is simply profit that is lost due to the unavailability of a resource.

Does the problem require further investigation?

Occasionally, some members of the problem-team may have some concerns that require further investigation or explanation. It is also common to put these items on a project, or a ***to-do-list***, to resource at a later time. Sometimes, it is not feasible due to various reasons such as available resources and potential impacts to conduct these experiments or investigations. This is also your opportunity to correctly analyze all the data for clarification.

What other issues were uncovered during your plan?

As stated throughout this book, it is unacceptable to tolerate poor performing systems or processes. If left alone, these systems will begin to deplete your profit margins. **TAKE** the time to review all documented work performed to uncover hidden opportunities. It's your responsibility as the problem-owner to ensure that all the observations and actions performed are fully comprehended. Develop a plan if necessary.

Are there any unanswered questions?

A problem is not truly solved until the root-cause is fully understood. Oftentimes when egos are not checked at the door, root-causes are not always agreed upon by everyone on the problem team. *Brainstorm your conclusions*. It is important to attempt to answer all the questions that could cloud the understanding of a root-cause. Improper troubleshooting techniques such as ***shot-gunning, easter-egging*** *or* ***swaptronics*** usually contribute to the failure to agree upon what the problem or root-cause really was. Problem teams that settle with this approach are destined to repeat this problem again. If the correct actions are not taken to mitigate this problem, it will return. The data must support your conclusion or model. Often an experiment or test may need to be conducted to support your conclusions. However, sometimes it is not feasible or cost-effective to prove some theories.

Are all assigned tasks to mitigate this problem completed?

This is extremely important to understand. Many problems could have been avoided if someone would have only completed the task that they were assigned during a problem evaluation. It is extremely embarrassing to have a problem repeat itself because someone neglected to complete his/her assigned task to sustain a solution.

True Story: The Wrong Part

During one such problem evaluation, we discovered that a wrong part was used during a problem-solving effort. The problem originated at the equipment manufacturer; therefore it took a while to uncover. We also discovered that this was the second occurrence of this particular failure. Further investigation revealed that this faulty part was identified during the first occurrence. Unfortunately, no plans were developed to conduct an audit of the warehouse to physically remove these faulty parts from our supply system and return them back to the equipment manufacturer. As a result, the information became ***tribal knowledge****.*

What did your team learn about itself during the problem?

The team should have only one goal... to eliminate the problem and prevent it from reoccurring. Take this time to explore your approach to this problem. Try to understand what went wrong and what went right. Many problem teams disband prior to truly assessing their performance. If problems are not properly addressed or documented, it will come back to haunt you again. *Don't kid yourself.* Occasionally due to heated conversations, the *Problem Evaluation* phase is neglected all together. The idea being... *hey, we fixed the problem; that's all that should matter.*

Invest the time to attempt to conduct a thorough problem evaluation. Ensure that your sustaining solutions are completed or on track to completion. Dot all your *i's* and cross all your *t's*. Evaluate the highlights and lowlights of your team's performance. Rebuild relationships that may have been shaken during the problem-solving effort. Sometimes problem-solving can bring out the best and the worse in people. This meeting does not have to be formal. The conversation could occur over a cup of coffee. Once again, as the problem-owner it is your responsibility to create an atmosphere in which open and honest communication is valued and welcomed.

Summary: Phase 7 Problem Evaluation

- Evaluate the business impacts of your problem according to your stated objectives.

- Identify improvement opportunities that can be used as a learning tool for the next problem.

- Brainstorm your conclusions.

- Develop an experiment if necessary.

- Solve the ***A*** problems, before they become ***The*** problems of the future.

- Evaluate your team's overall performance.

- Conduct a detailed wrap-up of all the highlights and the lowlights of the process within your problem team.

Okay... now let's apply the *Problem Evaluation* phase to our heating problem.

We began this problem with no prior technical knowledge of how a gas heating furnace operated or how to troubleshoot the unit. We simply started with a problem that we were attempting to solve.

Did we meet our objectives and effectively implement countermeasures to prevent this problem from repeating itself? Did we truly solve the problem or did we simply place a *Band-Aid fix* in place only to repeat itself at a later date, right in the middle of winter? Finally, did we do what we said we would do?

Let's review our objectives:

- **Cost -** *Used the most cost-effective solution* - My total cost to repair the problem was $140 which was a cost avoidance of $1,860.

- **Time (schedule) -** *Minimum urgency* - Time was on my side. The temperatures were moderate. The heating system was up and running weeks before the full impact of winter was upon us.

- **Documentation -** *Major improvement required.*

    - **Theory of operation -** Created to explain how system is designed to operate.

    - **System block diagram -** Created to simplify system interactions.

    - **Process flow description** – Created to provide a step-by-step detailed description of the process.

- **Process flow chart** - Created to understand sequence of events.

- **Alarm interlock matrix** - Created to enable users to quickly identify system failures.

- **Brainstorming of faulty blower** – A faulty blower correlated with our problem description and data. During the initial troubleshooting effort it was noticed that the blower was constantly running during the summer months to force the cool air from the basement throughout the house. The system was placed in an operation mode which enabled the blower to remain constantly energized. This decision caused the blower to work harder than normal. The system has been in operation for five years without any blower errors. The failure mode aligns with an electrical/mechanical root-cause. The blower would operate for about two to four hours before coming to a complete controlled halt as though there was an electrical or mechanical breakdown. Further investigation ruled out the mechanical binding. After the blower was replaced, the system operation was noticeably quieter. It operated for eight hours without any problems. Upon error-free operation for 48 hours, I declared the system ready for the winter.

- **Behavior changes** - To extend the life of our new blower, we have made the decision to not run the blower full time. Especially during the winter months, because the cool air from the basement only cools the house down faster.

- **Fix the "A" problems now** - During the troubleshooting I also noticed that the filter was very dirty, preventing good clean air from circulating throughout the house. I purchased new filters to prevent poor circulation, overheating of components and to reduce the potential of respiratory problems for my family.

- **Provided Training** - I later sat the family down to provide some basic training regarding the proper operation and settings for our furnace system. I provided instructions on how to properly program the system to enable the system to operate in a safe cost effective mode.

Problem Evaluation
Problem Recognition
Problem Observation
Problem Analysis
Develop Solution
Validate Solution
Sustain Solution
Quick Review

Chapter 9

Quick Review

Success requires no apology.
- Unknown

Excellent job! You have completed the problem-solving process. Now you have been presented with some industry background, looming challenges, practical skills, and applicable strategies. It is my desire that you now have an increased level of confidence in your ability to manage your *day-to-day* problems; irregardless of how challenging they first appear. In this chapter we will conduct a *quick overview* of the key principles of each phase of this process.

The Anatomy of Problem-Solving Principles

1. **Problem Recognition** - Invest the time to accurately identify your problem. To increase the harmony within your problem team, carefully consider the skill sets that you need to effectively solve your problem prior to selecting the team members. Seek to fully understand how a system or process is designed to operate before you begin speculating about what is not functioning properly. *High agreement* will ensure that everyone is working on the same problem.

2. **Problem Observation** - In an unbiased approach, take the time to accurately observe the performance of the system or process. Record all your observations. Collect all the data that pertains to your problem. Conduct a thorough investigative approach to gain as much information as possible. Determine the frequency of the failure: *constant, intermittent or conditional*. Develop historical and failure analysis timelines of your problem.

3. **Problem Analysis** - Take the time to properly comprehend the data that you have collected. Attempt to put all the pieces of the puzzle together to develop some probable root-causes. ***The Data Don't Lie***. Resist the temptation to develop premature conclusions. Remember the *KISS* principle - don't over-analyze the data. ***It is what it is!*** For technical failures, characterize the nature of the failure as: electrical, mechanical, electronic, temperature or program related. Proactively address conflict when it arises in your team. Beware of team personalities problems.

4. **Develop Solution** - Develop and prioritize solutions that will satisfy your organization's objectives. Carefully customize your solutions and action plans to enable your team to safely and promptly obtain results.

5. **Validate Solution** - Execute plans in a manner that will enable you to accurately determine the status and effects of your plans. Most problems are induced during this phase because of hasty and poor executions. ***Don't throw the baby out with the bath water.*** If first you don't succeed, try again. Carefully reevaluate your data and results. Proceed back through the process until you obtain complete resolution.

6. **Sustain Solution** – After the problem has been solved, it is equally important to implement solutions that will reduce the chances of the problem reoccurring in the future. Develop standards and documentations for all too fully benefit from the new knowledge. Eliminate the threat of ***tribal knowledge***. Every problem is a learning opportunity. Protect your new information with proper documentation.

7. **Problem Evaluation** - Review the problem to better comprehend how your team performed. Make sure that all assumptions are sound. Brainstorm your conclusions.

Verify that all assigned tasks were completed or at least scheduled to be completed at some future date.

This process works every time! It may take you a little longer to make this a habit, but it will be well worth the time invested. Resist the temptation to exclude phases in this process. In doing so, you will usually only prolong and frustrate your efforts. As I stated previously, ***your ability to effectively solve problems is in direct proportion to your ability to be successful in any career you choose.*** This proven approach has been the key to my success as a technician, engineer, project leader, and consultant. I approach all problems with confidence.

Problem
Evaluation
Problem
Recognition
Problem
Observation
Problem
Analysis
Develop
Solution
Validate
Solution
Sustain
Solution
Why Should You Care?

Chapter 10

Why Should You Care?

As long as we feel victimized,
we give up the power to change.
- Unknown

It is my opinion that effective problem-solving is slowly becoming a lost art in many industries. The true cost of equipment downtime is shrinking the profit margins of many companies. In response, companies are forced to reduce their operation cost to satisfy apprehensive stockholders. Many companies are aggressively reducing headcount, moving jobs overseas, and deciding to close non-profitable operations. It is imperative for those who desire to be successful in today's high-tech competitive environment to be able to effectively solve problems in a team environment.

True Story: DIA - United Airlines' Baggage System

To further prove my position regarding the lost art of troubleshooting, as of June 7, 2005, United Airlines officially announced their plans to abandon one of the world's most advanced automated baggage systems. They were unable to solve the many technical problems that plagued the Denver International Airport (DIA) since it first opened in 1995. The automated debacle cost ***$240M to construct.*** *The original builder BAE Systems constructed three similar systems prior to this system.* ***The City of Denver paid an additional $431M to try to repair*** *the electrical-mechanical automated nightmare that continued to chew-up customer luggage and cause severe cart jams and derailments.*

The City of Denver leases the system to United Airlines who filed for Chapter 11 Bankruptcy protection. Under the bankruptcy agreement, United Airlines has to pay the City of Denver ***$60M over 25 years*** *for the failed system. The debacle was responsible for repeated delays for United Airlines. Abandoning this system saves the company* ***$1M dollars per month*** *that it pays to technicians who maintain this system (in other words... people will lose their jobs). United has also had to leap many legal hurdles due to lawsuits before finally admitting that this system has been* ***a thorn in the flesh*** *from the beginning. DIA is regarded as one of the worst airports in the country for timely departures. The airline has announced plans to fully convert to a traditional conveyor manual system in 2007. (Nguyen, 2005)*

United Airlines' failed automated system will serve as a model example to many upcoming project managers, of what happens when a project is poorly executed. This project was doomed to fail from the beginning due to poor planning and communication. For example, the initial airport design did not take into consideration that this system had been selected. As a result, BAE tried to develop a system (work-around) according to the airport's already designed luggage tunnels. Also, due to schedule delays, the system was never fully tested before full implementation.

The Data Don't Lie

The data is difficult to dispute. The media is beginning to regularly report alarming statistics regarding the upcoming *skill-shortage gap* throughout industries in the U.S. Many analysts are publicly debating the sensitive issue of losing American jobs to other countries. Advanced industrialized countries such as China are reportedly graduating more engineers than the U.S. Many analysts are reporting that the problem is not going to be a lack of jobs in the U.S., but rather a lack of skilled-workers to fill these positions. Though we invest more dollars per student, the U.S. education test scores are continuing to fall behind other advanced industrialized nations. Recent surveys are also reporting that recent college graduates of 2 and 4 year colleges are failing to achieve proficient literacy and quantitative skills. College students are reported to spend more money for alcohol than books. Every year more undergraduates will die from alcohol-related causes than will graduate with masters and PhD's combined. Regularly, we are hearing about many disturbing incidents that are occurring on our college campuses such as sexual assault and drug-related crimes. Currently, we are also hearing more and more K-12 teachers molesting their students. One must ask…what is going on? Armed with these statistics many advocates are lobbying for a total over-haul of our K-12 and college education system. They declared that our education system is simply out of touch with our upcoming challenges.

The U.S. high-tech manufacturing sector is also being impacted as a direct result of these *skill-shortage gaps*. Coupled with an aging workforce, many companies are reporting having difficulties locating and retaining the premium higher level skilled-workers to give their companies the competitive advantage they desire. It is becoming common news for companies to announce a major recall of a product due to defects that escaped their quality control systems. These losses are sometimes difficult to overcome forcing many companies to close their doors, thus causing more Americans to be out of work. Many of these workers are not fully prepared to re-enter the highly competitive and highly technical industries due to *out-dated skills*. The continued globalization of our economies will prompt many U.S. companies to expand their operations off-shore to be more competitive. Trying to satisfy volatile industry demands in a *Just-In-Time* manufacturing environment with a looming shortage of skilled-workers will be the number one priority for many manufacturing companies to solve.

High technology companies are finding it more difficult to maintain the lucrative profit margins of recent years. The majority of the high-tech industry products fall within discretionary spending categories. Unlike a home and utilities such as gas and electricity, customers don't really need to purchase high-tech products such as fancy cell phones, laptops, plasma TVs, etc. Most of the high-tech products are considered to be *nice-to-haves;* most of us can live without them. As a result, the demand for high-tech products is affected by the consumers' confidence in the economy and the job market. Also, the intense competition within the high-tech industry has exacerbated many companies' ability to remain profitable by evoking deep cutting price wars. However, this is great news for savvy consumers. In response, high-tech companies are becoming more creative in their marketing strategies and product mix to satisfy this new awakening of the consumer.

Facing the same economic challenges of low product demands, lower average selling prices for products, high fixed capital for items such as building and expensive manufacturing facilities, reducing variable cost is the only area of improvement that many companies have to remain competitive. Variable/operational cost is the expenditure associated with the cost of doing business. Variable cost includes: employee salaries, inventory, spare parts, raw materials, training and routine maintenance etc. Operation cost is an easy target for most financial managers. As a result, reducing headcount and funds for training are usually the first to be impacted as the company attempts to become leaner.

Although this will give you immediate results; in the long-run most companies usually cut too deep, thus loosing valuable employees and skill sets. These policies serve only as a temporary containment strategy. The real problem for companies to solve is their inabilities to effectively solve business/technical problems and to discover practical opportunities to continue to out-perform their competition. Comprehending the economic affects in your industry and how to respond will be paramount to your success as a professional problem-solver.

Along with their core career competencies, the next generation of problem-solvers will require strong leadership skills and the ability to effectively solve problems in a team environment. We must continually learn to be innovators to remain competitive. The job market will require more of them. We must give the current and next generation of problem-solvers the tools and confidence to be successful. Effectively solving problems in a team environment will be the competitive advantage for many companies who desire to meet the challenges of the future.

Final Thoughts

Now, I hope you truly comprehend why you need to take the subject matter of this book very seriously. It would behoove you to begin to apply this problem-solving approach to all that you do, especially when it relates to technical, business, and project problems. I have provided you with the collected knowledge and wisdom that I have acquired throughout my career as a professional technical team problem-solver. It was my goal to apply some humor and practicality to the subject. Throughout this book, it was my desire to offer you some practical strategies that can be applied to your everyday problem-solving challenges. It was also my intent to provide you with some thought provoking true stories and quotes to help you navigate through your career as a professional problem-solver.

As a veteran problem-solver of 20-years, I have never deviated from this approach that I learned when I was 18. I approach every problem in the same manner, irregardless of how big or small it appears. I can scale my approach according to the problems that I encounter. With the correct resources available and patience, I can usually go through the process quickly with absolute accuracy.

I have enjoyed writing this book. In doing so, it has allowed me to deposit into you the wisdom that was deposited into me ~20 years ago as a young, anxious teenager. I have had the privilege to sit at the feet of some excellent problem-solvers. It is now up to you to embrace the concepts in this book as the foundation of your career. I'm confident that the principles of *The Anatomy of Problem-Solving* will enable you to become all that you purpose in your heart.

References

Baldi, Stephan. American Institute for Research. January 2006. *New Study of the Literacy of College Students Finds Some Are Graduating with only Basic Skills.* http://www.air.org/news/documents/Release200601pew.htm

Cole, Edwin Louis. (1995). *Manhood 101. How to be Man of Courage and Integrity in a World of Compromise.* ISBN 1562920510

Elmasry, Faiza. July 2005. *College Graduates Prepare for Job Market.* http://www.voanews.com/english/archive/2005-07/2005-07-29-voa34.cfm

Leonard, Joel. Pulse Point Technology. (2005). *The Cost of Ignorance.* http://www.bin95.com/news/proactive_ solution.htm

Messmer, Max. (1996). *Steer Clear of Skill Gaps.* http://www.workforce.com/archive/article/22/02/52.php

NACE. 2005. Job Outlook 2005. http://www.jobweb.com/joboutlook/2005outlook/3a.htm

National Associations of Manufactures. 2001. *Shortage of Skilled Workers Imperils the Industry.* http://www.nam .org/s_nam/doc1.asp?CID=201910&DID=231629

Nguyen, Kim. Associated Press. June 2005. *United Airlines to Ditch Troubled Automated Baggage System.* http://www.compliancepipeline.com/164301316

US Department of Labor. *Census of Fatal Occupational Injuries 2005.* http://www.bls.gov/iif/oshwc/cfoi/cftb0207.pdf

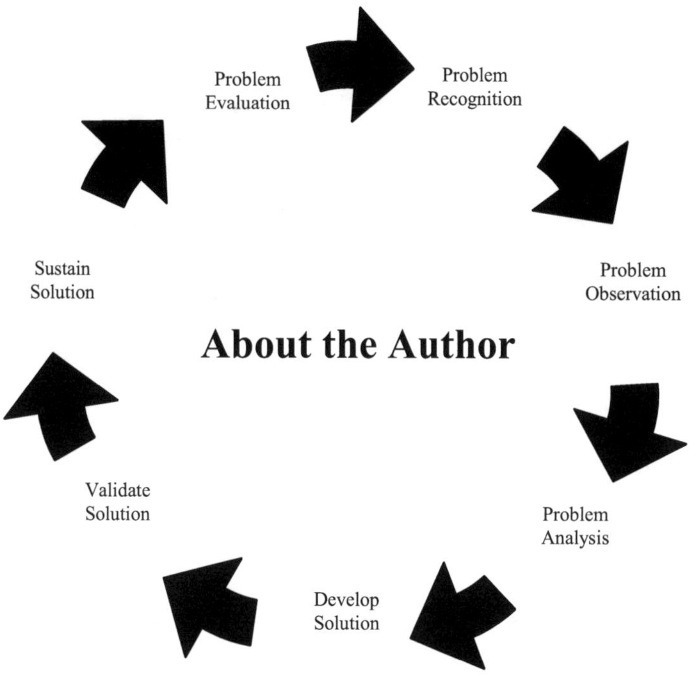

About the Author

About the Author

Tim Hobbs started his career as a technical problem-solver in the US Navy. During his tenure, he managed various highly advanced naval electronic systems. He was also assigned to a ship repair facility in Pearl Harbor, Hawaii, which enabled him to solve various problems in a timely manner that generally eluded his peers. He received many awards including three Naval Achievement Awards for his keen ability to solve some very difficult problems in an innovative and effective manner. At the young age of 19, he was awarded the highly sought after *Sailor of the Year* award at his first command in Keflavik, Iceland where he discovered his problem-solving talent.

With over nine years of faithful service, Tim decided to end his naval career to spend more time with his family. Prior to his departure from the Navy, he obtained an associate's degree from Honolulu Community College. He later decided to pursue a career in the high-tech manufacturing industry as a manufacturing technician. Though new to the industry, he was able to command the attention of his interviewers during his first interview. So impressed with his ability to solve problems, he was offered a position as a senior technician 10 months before his departure from the Navy. Eager to learn, Tim spent the first year learning the complexities of the high-tech manufacturing industry. Immediately, he was able to begin to solve some of the industry's most complicated problems using his proven problem-solving approach. He soon became the envy of his peers and engineers. In a matter of hours, he was literally solving problems that had plagued his teams for days, weeks and sometimes months.

He later set his eyes back on higher education in which he received a Bachelor in Science in Information Systems and a MBA in Technology Management from the University of Phoenix. He was later promoted to an Equipment Engineer. In this role, he led many successful problem-solving efforts and engineering projects.

In response to persistent requests of his colleagues, Tim decided to write *The Anatomy of Problem-Solving* to enable others to learn and benefit from his experience and success as an expert problem-solver. He is the president and founder of Hobbs Technical Consulting, LLC. He is an in-demand problem-solver and keynote motivational speaker. He trains organizations and professional groups how to effectively solve problems in a team environment through his seminars and workshops. His mission is to train the next generation of professional problem solvers. *The Anatomy of Problem-Solving Professional Workshop* is an approved college accredited workshop from the University of Colorado, Colorado Springs (UCCS). To learn more information regarding upcoming events of the workshops and seminars please visit www.hobbstech.com.

Tim has an innate passion to help others succeed. He is a member of the University of Colorado, Colorado Springs (UCCS) College of Education Dean's Advisory Board. He is also an adjunct professor at UCCS. In 2006, he was awarded the President's Volunteer Service Award for his strong community involvement. He has been married to his wife for over 15 years and has three wonderful children. His family resides in beautiful Colorado Springs, Colorado.

Made in the USA